Now I Read Me Down to Sleep
(Calvin's Perspectives)

Calvin S. Metcalf

Mossy Creek Press

Now I Read Me Down to Sleep
ISBN: Softcover 978-1-951472-84-9
Copyright © 2015 by Calvin S. Metcalf

All rights reserved. No part of this book may be reproduced or transmitted in any form or by any means, electronic or mechanical, including photocopying, recording, or by any information storage and retrieval system, without permission in writing from the publisher.

Biblical scripture references taken from the following translations:

King James Version
New King James Version
New American Standard Bible
New International Version

To order additional copies of this book, contact:
Mossy Creek Press
1-423-475-7308
www.mossycreekpress.com

Mossy Creek Press is an imprint of Parson's Porch & Company (PP&C) in Cleveland, Tennessee. PP&C is an innovative organization which raises money by publishing books of noted authors, representing all genres. All donations from contributors and profits from publishing are shared with the students of Carson – Newman University.

Now I Read Me Down to Sleep
(Calvin's Perspectives)

Table of Contents

Preface	13

Timely Perspectives

A Place of Beginning Again	17
The Stewardship of Time	18
The Inner Child of Our Past	19
Enchantment or Commitment	20
Ageless Beauty	21
A Reflective Prayer	22
God's Promised Eternity	23
Hope and Dreams	24
The Unknown	25
On Being Human	26
Anticipation	28
God's World	29
Change	30
Hallelujah!! Amen.	31
Getting Away	32
The Challenge of Change	33
Time-Wise	34
Walking With God	36
The Sabbath Principle	38
Transcendence and Presence	40
The Good Old Days	41
Being Alive	42
A Timely Prayer	43
Forward Through the Ages	44
Peace with Our Past	45
Growing Through Risk	46
"Been There, Done That"	48
Busy Boredom	50
Growing Old with Grace	51
What are We Dying for?	52
Death in Gospel Perspective	54
Death Defying Faith	56

Biblical Perspectives

Finding Our Song	59
Secrets	60
Reflecting God's Love	62
Listening Ears	63
Gospel Economics	65
Prejudice	66
Economic Security	67
Who then is Holy?	68
Keepership	69
God's Ways	71
The Beatitudes	72
Religious Intimidation	73
A Father's Lament	74
Inner Music	76
Coloring Outside the Lines	77
Growing Through Adversity	78
His Presence, Our Peace	79
Is This All There Is?	80
Love's Power	81
On Being Consistent	82
Poverty	83
The Bible	84
The Father's Will	85
Holy Bible, Book Devine	86
Biblical Integrity	87
Being Fed by Feeding	88
God's Power	89
Cleverness	90
Religious or Righteous	91
Imagination	92
Vengeance	93
Truth or Consequences	94
Mysteries	95
Spiritual Recovery	96
The Will of God	97
Holy Bible	98
"Agape" Love	99
Something for Nothing	100
Suspicion	101
Simon and Thomas	102

A Strong Case for Heaven	103
Wonderful Words of Life	104
Getter or Giver	105
The Word of God	106
Mumblings of a Christian Jew	107
Martha and Mary	109
Spirit-Led Conclusions	110
Jacob's Well	112
The Privilege of Prayer	105

Community Perspectives

A Worship Thought	118
Called to Participate	119
The Gift of Work	121
Education versus Indoctrination	122
God's Diversity	123
Money	124
On Being Family	125
People Power	126
Picky People	127
Defining Neighbor	128
Communication	129
Church Burnout	131
Church-Worthy Trust	133
People Adjustments	134
Comfort	135
Despisory Vs Respectory	136
Dinner's Ready	137
Priests	138
War and Peace	139
A Missionary Moment	140
Kindness	141
Enemies	142
Giving Others Power over Us	144
Hunger	145
Worship	146
Reconciliation	147
Guilt Trips	148
Disfranchisement	149
Friendship	151
Love and Freedom	152

Commissioned	153
Caring For Others	154
A Prayer of Searching	155
A Prayer of Unity	156
Two or Three Gathered	157
The Risk of Ministry	158
Church	160
Contagious	161
Virtues That Protect	162
Polarities and Problems	163
"Amazable"	165
Church and State	166
Church Invaluable	167

Personal Perspectives

Why?	171
Jealousy	172
Right and Wrong	174
Anger	175
Joy	176
The Sheep Lesson	177
Affluenza	178
Doubt	179
A Miracle	180
A Closed Mind	181
Motive	182
Escape the Gloom	184
Silver or Rusty Spoons	186
The Christian Advantage	188
Memories	189
Confidence	190
Forgiveness	191
Learning to Like Ourselves	192
Perception	194
Hunger for the New	195
Know Thyself	196
For the Loving God	198
Heart Trouble	200
Being Oneself	202
Personal Hostility	203
Finding Our Potential	205

Close Minds, Hard Hearts	206
Good Guilt	207
Responding to Despair	208
Integrity	209
Put on a Happy Face	210
Dealing with Dislike	212
Sin Made Easy	213
Our Story	214
Grace Abuse	215
Secret Hideaway	216
Learning to Survive	217
Forgetfulness	218
Prayerograph	219
Struggling Faith	220
Painful Servanthood	221
Pride	222
Disposition	223
In the Beginning, God	224
Scars	226
Conviction with Courtesy	227
The God of Our Imagination	228
Our Way of Seeing Things	229
Patience	231
Dealing with Spontaneity	232
Olympic Faith	234

Seasonal Perspectives

Autumn Leaves	237
Thanksliving	238
The Christmas Event	239
Celebrating Christmas	240
Lights	241
Presence in Our Presents	242
Receivers and Givers	244
After Christmas Letdown	245
A Prayer for Year's End	246
Happy Endings	247
The New Year	248
Ambition	249
Life	250
The Death of Jesus	251

The Resurrection	252
Resurrection Thoughts	253
The Resurrection Event	254
Thomas (An Easter Monologue)	255
No Cross, No Crown (Soliloquy)	257
Bread and Cup	258
God in the Ordinary	259
Success and Failure	260
The Unity of God	262
Ode to a Mother	264
Fatherhood	265
Patriotism	266
Love Will Prevail	267
Bringing Out the Best	268
More than Luck	269
The Pronouncement of Work	271

Future Perspectives

Prayer of Positive Thought	275
The Future in Perspective	276
About the Author	277

Acknowledgments

My deepest appreciation goes to my wife, Bobbie, who assisted in every aspect of this book, and to my sister, Myra Hall, who assisted in typing and proofreading. I am also grateful to all who encouraged me to give my newspaper column entitled "Another Perspective" a larger readership.

The book is dedicated to the memory of my dear grandson, Jonathan Metcalf, who left us far too early because of a fatal accident. His memory lingers as an inspiration to all who enjoyed his vibrant personality.

Calvin was unable to see this book to completion. His family worked closely with others in establishing a proper format to submit for publication.

Preface

Sleep is a vital aspect of our health and wellbeing. Without quality sleep our nervous system breaks down and we become less productive. When sleep is interrupted, spasmodic, or denied for any reason our happiness and sense of wellbeing are affected. Sleep is one thing on our schedule of life that is required. We cannot fudge on this time of nocturnal rest and be a wholesome, healthy person. It is a violation of our created purpose to minimize the opportunity for peaceful, restful and consistent sleep. People who ignore or mistreat this special time are usually tense, anxious and hard to live with.

Sleep specialists give us many suggestions for the improvement of our sleep. One of the things they explore is the effect of what we are doing, reading or watching on television before going to bed. Sometimes a highly emotional movie, disturbing ten o'clock news or a family argument can play havoc with our sleep. These experts seem to be suggesting that we have something more emotionally and spiritually comforting on our minds as we lay ourselves down to sleep.

Here, then, is the purpose of this little book entitled "NOW I READ ME DOWN TO SLEEP." It is designed to meet our need for spiritual thoughts and create a wholesome mood for sleep.

Hopefully as one reads one of these devotionals prior to bedtime it will add to the quality of his or her sleep.

As children we said our bedtime prayers to create a mood for peaceful sleep. As adults we need a similar quieting of our minds to face the challenges that often hinder the quality of our sleep as well as the productivity of our lives. If the last thing on our minds at bedtime is a thought from these pages we may find rest for our weary souls. If such should happen then the goal of this book will have been fulfilled.

As the psalmist wrote so eloquently in Psalms 4:8 "In peace I will both lie down and sleep, for thou alone, O Lord, dost make me to dwell in safety."

Timely Perspectives

A Place of Beginning Again

Life is an interesting study in beginnings and endings. God, in His creative wisdom, has chosen to set limits on our earthly conditions. Human circumstances and events do not last forever. Things run their course and they are over. Life is a series of starts and finishes. The New Year begins, spends its days and months and then it ends. A child is born, lives out the proverbial three-score years and ten, and then dies. Time moves on with its inevitable changes. We continually adjust to the openings and closings of life's accounts. We seem to be obsessed with a need for things to stay the same and when they do not, we are sad. Even happy endings give us a sense of anxiety because of the challenge of new possibilities.

The routines of life are often terrible taskmasters because of our commitment to the way things are. Because of life's beginnings and endings, there is an interesting flexibility to the way we must live. Old patterns and schemes of doing things must give rise to the dawning of new ideas. It seems that life has a terrible capacity for innovation, which leaves us with a variety of choices. We are often confused at the crossroads, trying to decide which direction leads to the most happiness. At times, we wish life were more predictable and would not confront us with the trauma of decision. We want God to violate the creative process and make things last forever. Yet, life keeps on changing and we are compelled either to grow or to growl. We can find God in the midst of life's variety, or we can get lost in our dogged determination to keep things as they are.

There is, however, a redemptive aspect to change. The fact that things do not stay the same means that we do not have to stay the way we are. There is a way to end those things which have been damaging and destroying the vitality of life. There is A PLACE OF BEGINNING AGAIN with God as the focus of whatever adjustments we have to make to life's changes. The principle of change means we do not suffer forever, the new can be better than the old, and all things can work together for good if we love God.

The Stewardship of Time

Time moves on with each ticking of the clock, each winding of the watch and each turning of the calendar. Life moves on with each beat of the heart, each journey completed and each goal achieved. The past is memory and the future is hope. There is no way to change the scheme of things. We simply adjust to the patterns of our existence. Life is not so much a matter of altering circumstances as it is a matter of altering attitudes. The passing of time is inevitable. The longer we live the less likely we will live much longer. The key to happiness is not found in the amount of time lived, but in the quality of time given to the things that really matter. Age is relative. Whatever is left of us in terms of time and energy can be productive if we are committed to the best that is within us. God does not hand us life on a silver platter. We are created with a freedom to make the most or the least out of what happens to us.

Time is the stuff out of which life is made, and it can be either our enemy or our friend. We have the capacity to make it harmful or helpful. For example, it takes time to become a reprobate. It takes time to become addicted to evil's cunning devices. It takes time to sin away our spiritual birthrights. It takes time to develop a hateful disposition. It takes time to nurture our hates and hostilities. It takes time to make enemies.

On the other hand, it takes time to be holy. It takes time to develop our walk with God. It takes time to cultivate a disposition of grace. It takes time to learn the lessons of love and forgiveness. It takes time to do unto others, as we would have them do unto us. It takes time to make friends and have a godly influence. It takes time to fulfill our highest hopes. It takes time to be in love with life. It takes time to make time our friend.

The stewardship of time, therefore, is one of life's most demanding requirements. We cannot treat time as though we have an inexhaustible supply of it. There are precious moments to be guarded and there are difficult times to be endured. There are happy days to celebrate and sorrowful events to mourn. Being good stewards of time means that we learn and grow as we adjust to whatever life imposes upon us. Faith prepares us for the unexpected. Love gives us a new lease on life. Hope anticipates God's glorious tomorrow. Worship enables us to fit the pieces of life's puzzle into the time frame of our allotted days.

The Inner Child of Our Past

Underneath our tough and successful adult exterior there continues to beat the heart of a child. This child, which we once were, has blended into the pattern of our maturity and still reaches out for love, acceptance, and attention. Even though we may have put away some childish things, the inner child of our past is a present reality. Those inferiorities and fears of childhood days continue to influence our adult behavior. Those lessons learned and truths accepted as a child form the basis of our moral and ethical judgments today. The commitments made and the faith expressed as a child give stability and strength to our adult character. Likewise the hurts and problems of childhood and adolescence have a lingering effect upon our personalities. We are the product of all that has transpired since the beginning days of our lives.

We cannot fully escape the influences of our early years. We do not shed our childhood skin and suddenly become an adult. We cannot borrow from another's past. For better or for worse we live in the context of our own personal history. Sometimes this requires emotional and spiritual adjustments.

Here again the grace of God is our greatest ally, as we trust Him for guidance toward maturity. He can take the formative influences of our lives and mold them into a growing faith. Jesus called it "rebirth" and it means, when necessary, we can escape what time has done to us. It is possible, in Christ, for the inner child of the past to have a positive effect upon our adult happiness. Being "born again" gives us a place to start over as we put the past episodes of our lives into the context of healing grace. The child, which we once were, can blend into the adult, which we now are.

No doubt in the eyes of our heavenly Father we are always children at some stage of mental and spiritual development. Could it be that His basic word to us is that we suffer the child which we are to come unto Him, for of such is the kingdom of heaven? After all, it is as a child we come, no matter what our age.

Enchantment or Commitment

Sometimes it seems that God offers little help in the midst of our troubles. We pray for His specific intervention, and often the desired results are not in keeping with our expectations. We want Him to fix our lives and cure our spiritual ailments. We plead with Him to adjust events and circumstances so that our lot in life is more favorable. When our desired goals are not achieved, we tend to turn upon God as though He were the culprit who designed our defeat. We want instant solutions to complicated problems as if God were obligated to make our fairyland dreams come true. Even in our prayers, we try to put pressure on God to accommodate our success and prosperity.

Why is it that we cannot accept the seeming silence of God as a part of His loving plan for our lives? For one thing, we may have overlooked the fact that God calls out the best that is within us. We are challenged by the happenings of life to think, to pray, to act and to grow. We can never expect God to do for us what we are able, yet unwilling, to do for ourselves.

Another factor, which contributes to our disappointment, is an unrealistic relationship with God. There is a strong difference between an "enchantment" with God and a "commitment" to the ways of God. We tend to find the miraculous only in the spectacular and the noisy, forgetting that God still speaks through the "still small voice" of life's common events. "Commitment" waits for God's timetable while "enchantment" becomes nervous over God's delayed reactions. Faith is still the key to abundant living. The ability to trust God's loving purpose, even amid discouragement and defeat, is life's most rewarding disposition. In this sense, faith is the victory that overcomes the world. Our most humble and worthy prayer is "Lord, I believe, help thou my unbelief."

Ageless Beauty

Aging is a process that has a profound effect upon all of us. From the youngest to the oldest of us it creates a need for adjustments. Young folk who cannot wait to get older have to accept the slowness of the process. Older people who mourn the passing years have to adjust to the way time flies. Life has a way of presenting a variety of challenges and opportunities as we move in and out of each phase of the aging process. We are not always in control of the physical factors of growing older, but we can develop a disposition, which makes the adjustments easier. We can either deny or accept the journey toward life's sunset. We can become either bitter or better as we monitor the passing of time. Deep down we know it is better to celebrate the stages of life than to resent them. We know that aging is inevitable and the better equipped we are to face it the easier we make the transitions it requires.

In many ways the circumstances of life keep us in touch with ourselves. Faith along the journey keeps us hopefully anticipating the view from the next hill we climb. Love from those and for those who walk beside us energizes us for every emergency. Forgiveness and grace keep us close to the things of God. Serving the Lord even as we serve one another gives us the joy of productive living. Heartache and sorrow can sweeten our sensitivities. Self-esteem can keep us from looking back with morbid regret. Humility can help us seek a more excellent way. A submissive spirit can be the reward of years.

Let us, therefore, "Grow lovely growing older. There are so many fine things to do." Time may take its toll on physical beauty, but inner attractiveness thrives with the passing years. Time may slow the pace, but experience adds wisdom to the maturing years. We learn as we live even as we learn to live. Aging has much to teach us if we stop to smell the roses. Life is lived a day at a time, but the accumulation of days gives us a sense of history. We are part of something bigger than ourselves. Aging is God's design for humankind. In Him we find the mental and spiritual preparation for growing older. In Him we find "the last of life for which the first was made."

A Reflective Prayer

O Lord my God, You are a mighty being. I celebrate Your creative ingenuity. I marvel at the mystery of Your ways and the power by which You perform Your purpose. You have made me with a capacity to be curious and for that reason I am filled with wonder and awe. My eager imagination causes me to reflect upon how it might have been in the beginning.

From my limited human perspective, I imagine You busying Yourself with creation's chores. I can see You flinging stars, moon and sun into their places and putting planets into their orbits as You decorate the heavens for centuries of celestial observation.

In my mind's eye I see You selecting planet earth as a special garden to express the beauty of Your creative skills. I observe You spinning it around the sun in such a way that its seasons offer heat and health for all kinds of living things. I see You setting in motion a variety of laws and principles, which my most scientific thoughts have yet to grasp. I imagine You calling forth all the elements of earth and arranging them in geometric continuity. I see You looking out over Your created order and You are pleased.

The beauty, which my imagination is able to behold, is limited only by my lack of vision. I stop short of seeing ultimate reality because sin and time have dulled my senses. As I watch You moving amid that which You have made, I detect a note of loneliness. You have no one with whom to share Your marvelous universe. I wonder what is going through Your mind. And then I see you bend over and tenderly form a bit of dust into Your own image. You breathe into that lifeless form the breath of life and it becomes a living being. A smile comes across Your face and then a sense of sadness. You have created humankind who can give You delight but may also give you grief.

You are God and You are glory. I praise You because I am wonderfully made. But who am I that You are mindful of me? Who am I to have the benefit of Your inspired thoughts? Who am I to deserve this breath of life and this moment of grace? Who am I to think I could even imagine creation's mystery? Help me to be your humble servant who longs not only to dream about You, but to dream with You.

God's Promised Eternity

The mystery of time is surpassed only by the mystery of eternity. Time, as we know it has beginning and end. It has definable boundaries. Eternity has no beginning and no end. Because we live in time we are conditioned by the limitations of that which is temporary and perishable. Our thought processes are not equipped to think in terms of that which is everlasting and eternal. We reach into that realm of existence by faith. It is the vision of the heart and the eyes of the soul, which look into the land of forever and ever. We search for words because our vocabularies are limited as we try to discuss that which is timeless. "Infinity" is a word we seldom use because we know so little about it.

The scriptures give us a hint of heaven, yet the only thing we know for sure about it is we shall be with God. Of course that is enough, but our exploring minds try to envision what heaven will be like. We finger lovingly those passages, which contain vision and suggestion about the hereafter. Although Bible writers used earth's most precious objects to describe heaven, we still live with the reality that it has not entered human minds all God has in store for His people.

However, this does not mean we should give no thought to that which is eternal. It is important to let our imaginations explore that which is immortal. It stretches our minds to reflect upon that which is ultimate. It is a matter of faith that we have any interest at all in God's promised eternity. Indifference about everlasting life most likely reveals a carelessness about earthly life. The point to ponder is the awesome relation between the two. We go on living in the hereafter on the basis of how we live in the here and now. There is an eternal dimension to life that we do well not to ignore even though it surpasses our most disciplined thoughts.

We must never let a lazy mentality keep us from looking deep into the mysteries of whatever lies before us. While living in time, let us, therefore, look beyond the temporal to that which is permanent and eternal. It is another way to reflect upon God and His glory.

Hope and Dreams

Somewhere the past meets the future, and most of us struggle somewhere in between wondering if "what has been" has to be reproduced in the "what can be." Can the present moment be transformed by hope, or do dreams die when crushed by reality? Does our sense of expectancy lie dormant waiting for something sensational to revive it? Is tomorrow always defined in terms of yesterday? To anticipate the future is horror if the past has left no basis for our dreams. How can we live if, somehow from some source, we are not encouraged to believe and to trust in God's creative concern for our wellbeing and peace of mind? There must be a legitimate cause to keep on if for no other reason than to keep on keeping on.

The lessons of life are hard to learn. The school of discipline and disappointment has assignments we often refuse. The dropout rate in life's obstacle courses is very high. If we are not careful, we will die long before our pulse rate stops. Where then do we get some positive affirmation that it is all right to be alive? In which direction do we turn if our journey seems to be headed down a dead-end street?

The Psalmist gives us a beautiful hope when he reminds us that, "The Lord is my light and my salvation, whom shall I fear? The Lord is the strength of my life; of whom shall I be afraid?" Somewhere in the context of our faith in God, we learn there is a love that will not let us go. We discover that the basis of our existence is for the delight of our God.

He has been pleased to create us in His image, and thus His will is that we be conformed to His Son. We are created with a capacity to dream His dreams and think His thoughts. In so doing, we develop a vibrancy of hope, which enables us to forget those thing, which are behind, and press on to the goal of God for our lives.

The Unknown

The unknown often holds frightening possibilities for most of us. We are paralyzed by the prospects of what seems to be an uncertain future. We are overwhelmed by that which we cannot adequately predict. We quickly lose our nerve in the midst of life's issues, which are not easily defined. We can accept that which is new if only there is more about it we can know. We can adjust to the challenge of the future as long as we are reasonably sure of its agenda. It is the mystery of life's uncharted channels that causes us stress. In the darkness of that which is yet undiscovered we long for a light to show us the way.

The truth of the matter is we have that light, and it shines as bright as the promises of God. It is a matter of faith that we are able to find meaning in the midst of the unexplainable. In the context of grace, we are able to see saving possibilities in the most awkward circumstances. In this life we are not equipped to know it all, but we do have a capacity to know something. We take that which we do know and face the unknown with courage.

We know that "God so loved the world," and we take that knowledge into the deepest mysteries of life. We know that Christ arose from the grave and in that knowledge we find security and hope for eternal life. We know that our Lord has a will and a purpose for all things. We, therefore, take comfort in His creative care.

We know that everything works for good to those who love Him and are called according to His purpose. We, therefore find meaning in all of life's circumstances.

The unknown will always be with us. The mystery of life will never be fully solved this side of eternity. In the meantime, however, we learn the value of trust as we walk in the light of God's loving revelation. Our ability to trust makes Him in whom we trust the object of our deepest devotion. "O God our help in ages past, our hope for years to come."

On Being Human

A great lesson every Christian needs to learn is that it is all right to be human. Now this does not mean it is all right to be sinful. Sometimes we get the two confused as we minimize our sins by the fact that we are "just human." We use the safety net of human frailty to rationalize our weaknesses. We almost blame God for our character flaws rather than assume any personal responsibility for our misdeeds. Although we are created in the image of God, we must address the weaknesses of the flesh with integrity and grace.

It is a theological and moral error to make our God-given humanity the scapegoat for all our transgressions. The truth of the matter is that being human and being sinful are not necessarily synonymous. Being human means it is all right not to know all the answers. It is all right to admit our spiritual weaknesses. It is all right to cry. It is all right to apologize and lean on each other for support. It is all right to confess our sins and seek forgiveness from God and whomever we may have offended.

Being human means that it is all right to lean on the everlasting arms of God and to resign as general manager of the universe. In fact, it is without question "more right" to be human, because the structure of our human personality cannot stand the strain of trying to play God. No doubt, we sin more in our attempt to be God than in our struggle with being human. We have far too much to learn about the dynamics of our own humanity before we begin taking lessons in the art of being divine.

Yet, we seem to be incurably possessed with the need to hate, to condemn, and to return evil for evil. We are forever trying to improve on what we perceive to be "God's creative blunders" as we seek to re-create everyone in our own image. Everyone who does not have our brand of spirituality and religious disposition is the object of our concern and sometimes the object of our scorn. Jesus calls us to love those we label as "enemy" which may mean to love those who are different. There is a lot of diversity in his kingdom.

Our greatest need may be that we relax our ambition to be judges and umpires of each other's lives. There is great relief when we grow to understand that "vengeance is mine, I will repay, saith the Lord." After all, being human means that we understand our common plight. We struggle to forgive and forget. We learn to be healers instead of agitators. Somewhere along life's journey we begin to accept our servant role as the best expression of our humanity.

Anticipation

Life is lived best with a sense of expectancy. We are prone to have a much healthier outlook when we have something to which we look forward. Hope is our greatest asset in developing an optimistic disposition. When we lose our ability to anticipate, we can easily become negative and critical. We lose our capacity to believe God can bring good out of evil. We fail to trust his ability to work in awkward situations and to use a variety of folk in performing his will. With no sense of expectancy, we tend to despair of life, assuming things are so bad even God offers little hope. It is a lack of faith that keeps us in bondage to a bleak interpretation of everything that happens to us.

While it is important for us to live in the real world, it is equally important for us to live, as it were, on tiptoe, always ready for whatever exciting adventure life may thrust upon us. With this sense of expectancy God can give us visions and dreams equal to our faith. When Jesus came to earth, he was received by a host of people who had lived with Messianic anticipation. For years, faithful Jews had expected God to intervene in some awesome event. It was these folk who formed the foundation on which our Lord Jesus built His church.

At first, they did not grasp the meaning of our Lord's mission. They wanted a more tangible kingdom where Messiah would not die but rule on earth in peace and prosperity. Their sense of expectancy, however, enabled them to see God's hand in things they could not fully understand. Their faith gave them the ability to celebrate what God had done and to anticipate what he might yet perform.

To those early Christians, no situation was hopeless. Circumstances did not have to please them before they plunged themselves into faithful obedience to their Lord. They served, believing that God could bring some good out of everything if they loved him and sought to fulfill his purpose. Therefore, like those first century Christians, let us keep our hopes high with a keen sense of expectancy that God is not finished with us yet and has many wonders to perform.

No one is happier than the person who can see God's light at the end of life's tunnel.

God's World

The glory of God's world is an often-neglected topic, not because we are unaware of it, but because we take it for granted. When we pause to consider the handiwork of the heavens with earth as God's wonderful footstool, we see majesty far beyond our comprehension. Beauty, which stretches our aesthetic imaginations, has theological implications we seldom explore. The involvement of a creator God in the intricate workings of nature is cause for worship and praise. The rhythm of the seasons, the clockwork of the universe and the precision of time and space confuse the mind of would-be atheists. It is sacrilegious to enjoy the beauty of the created order without the benefit of a belief in God. It is illogical to assume that such a magnificent universe occurred without divine planning.

Although it is pagan to worship nature, it is a matter of hope to see God in that which He has made. Let us never ignore the devotional possibilities in all of nature's events. The lightning flashes, the thunder rolls, the wind blows, the earth shakes as strong reminders that this is our Father's world. Let us never become so preoccupied with what transpires inside a man-made building that we ignore the larger sanctuary of God. To God be the glory, great things He has done.

What then is humankind that God is mindful of us? He has created us with a glory and honor of our own. It is not a status, which we have created or deserved. It is a stewardship of grace and a responsibility of love. We have no essential worth except that which is derived from this God of might and miracles. Why, then, should we be despondent, competitive and disagreeable? God has given us a tremendous world in which to move and live and have our being. We are its custodians and gardeners. We are the curators of its artifacts and the protectors of its precious resources.

Let us be about our divine assignments, lest we allow the clock of time to run down, and we have nothing left but a garbage heap. Surely, the Lord of creation will hold us responsible for this garden we've allowed to erode. Remember, it has the capacity to heal itself as well as those who tend it, if we cooperate with its laws and share its bounty.

Change

Change is an inevitable part of life's processes. We do not stay the same. We are forever moving either upward or downward, forward or backward. We do well to recognize our capacity for change and make the necessary adjustments along the way. We are created with an appetite for good and evil. The pull of both keeps us in transition. Life is a pilgrimage with a variety of visions on the journey. We must wisely monitor the things, which have the power to change us and make sure we are becoming the persons we want to be.

One of the most exciting pronouncements of the gospel is that we do not have to stay the way we are. There is a place to begin again. The old can be absorbed into the new. The bad can be transformed by the good. Repentance can be received. Forgiveness can be given. Restoration can occur. Nothing can be more personally satisfying than to sense a Godly renewing of our spirits. What a blessing it is to want a better walk by making plans to be a Jesus person. It does not happen all at once. The spiritual graph has its peaks and valleys. Highs and lows are a part of our pilgrimage. The human house is a strange combination of both success and failure. Our hope is in the fact that we do not have to remain stale and static. Change for the better is an ever-present possibility.

Of course the opposite is true. Regression is as much an option as progression. We are free to digress from our spiritual roots. We can choose to flirt with spiritual disaster. We can grow in disgrace as well as grace. Evil's appeal can lead us down the road of compromise. When this occurs our goals are tainted with iniquity. Our spiritual ambitions are sacrificed to whatever seems more expedient. We lose our will to want a better way. The menace of mediocrity keeps us from pursuing the best. Change for the worse is also a possibility.

Even though change is inevitable we have the capacity to choose the kind of changes we wish to make. No matter what our circumstances we are not locked into a predetermined lifestyle. It is constantly a matter of grace that God calls us onward and upward. Remember His grace is always sufficient.

Hallelujah!! Amen.

There are moments in life when it seems that God cooperates with any number of circumstances to give us a fresh vision of Himself. In our rather uneventful journey toward the future, we turn a corner and there is God. When this happens, prayer, which had once been perfunctory and dull, suddenly becomes productive. Our worship takes on the character of grace, inspiring us to have love for all kinds of people. The music of our souls seems to join the chorus of heaven in special celebration and praise. Our problems and perplexities are minimized in the presence of an all-sufficient God who maximizes our faith. It is a blessing, indeed, when the lights come on and we are able to see God and truth and people and life from a clearer perspective.

Life is full of spiritual surprises when we have eyes to see and ears to hear. The greatest tragedy, however, is our human capacity to miss the meaning of special moments. Sometimes the bush is burning and all we do is stand around and pick berries. The glory of the Lord is filling His holy temple and all we do is sit and grieve over our own personal agendas. The Lord Jesus wants to be born anew in our hearts, but we are busy, preoccupied and have no room. The resurrected Christ is making special appearances to His followers, but we are spiritually absent. The Damascus Road is happening, but for some reason, we have decided to go another way.

There is so much we can miss when we are not open and receptive to all God's truth. It is a matter of faith that we find God in our daily routine. The breeze of heaven is blowing upon the ordinary events of our lives. Let us reach out and touch the hem of His garment because Jesus is passing this way. Who knows what miracles await us when we replace resentment with repentance, confusion with confession and denial with dedication? And I heard a voice singing "Hallelujah!! Hallelujah!! AMEN."

Getting Away

Have you ever noticed that some resort centers and vacations sites are advertised as places "to get away from it all?" This is appealing to the general public because we all long for such a setting, which would enable us to escape life's mounting pressures. The prospects for a few days of quiet tranquil living is a dream with which most of us live. It almost becomes a part of the driving force that keeps us going. We work hard to afford that dream vacation or perhaps an early retirement to a place that will provide us peace and security.

In reality, there is no such place to get away from it all. We take our emotional and spiritual baggage with us. Whoever we are in the rush and responsibility of life is the same person who goes on retreat. Whatever idiosyncrasies beset us in the mainstream of life will likewise accompany us on vacation.

Peace of mind is not a place. It is a state of mind. "Getting away from it all" is more of a spiritual journey than a physical change of location. There is no value in travel if life's harassing agenda is left unresolved. Of course, a change of scenery helps, but only if it provides a setting for a new perspective.

Only God can equip us with the capacity for relaxation. In His forgiveness we find an escape from sin's burden of guilt. In Him we experience the beauty of reconciliation as we learn to forgive those who sin against us and to express repentance toward those we offend.

God can give us a healthy sense of values so we do not covet what others have. He enables us to be content with what we have and to find meaning in our material growth. Only in a calm commitment, of who we are and what we have, to Godly goals can we ever really get away from it all. We must seek first the kingdom of heaven and then we are spiritually prepared for a delightful trip to anywhere.

The Challenge of Change

Time marches on with each inevitable tick of the clock and turn of the calendar. How dependent we are on these devices, which monitor our days. Were there no such things as clocks and calendars, however, we still have many reminders of the passing of time. There is evidence all around us of what time is doing to us. We do not stay the same nor does our surroundings. Change is a significant aspect of our existence and we do well to accept it.

We either adjust to this fact or we lose ourselves in an attempt to live only in the past. In His creative wisdom, God has given us forward motion. The capacity to anticipate is one of life's great assets. While looking back can be a learning experience, the ability to dream and plan ahead is what allows us to grow.

How blessed we are when somehow, in the context of our faith, we assume a positive attitude toward the changes which time imposes upon us. It is indeed a dead-end street when we face the future with little or no hope. When change becomes our enemy instead of our servant, we lose a redeeming perspective on life.

The gospel encourages us to accept the challenge of change. We are commissioned to keep the faith, to fight the good fight and to anticipate God's presence in every circumstance. Jesus is Lord of the unknown as well as the known. He calls us on a journey, the path of which, we can only see by faith. His good news always has a future tense. The kingdom is always coming. In Christ Jesus tomorrow is always a day full of expectancy and hope.

Therefore, let us face the future with confidence that time is on our side and if we endure to the end we shall be saved. In love our Lord assures us that no defeat needs to be final, no obstacle needs to be permanent and no problem needs to remain unsolvable. So, have faith in God. He is on His throne yesterday, today and tomorrow.

Time-Wise

Time is a fascinating feature of our human existence. It is the stuff life is made of. We may lose some important items of life, but time is the most precious thing we could ever squander. We may be rich in worldly goods, but poor indeed if we have not time. Time is the context in which God created all things and allows history to record the events of His created order. We do well to redeem our time.

Our sins are often complicated because of the lack of time. We do not have enough time to make all the money we crave. We do not have enough time to satisfy all our ambitions. We do not have enough time to go all the places there are to go. We do not have enough time to make everyone our closest friend. We do not have enough time for all the available thrills and excitements in our world of entertainment.

We are often trapped by our perceived lack of time and it raises our frustration level to the point of indigestion. In our attempt to do it all today we overload our daily human capacities. We try to borrow so much today from tomorrow that if we are not careful we will bankrupt our souls before our years are spent.

Life is passing us by far more quickly than we can absorb it. The longer we live the less likely we will live any longer. Yet, many of us go on living our lives as if there will never be a change of schedule. We become fanatically committed to a routine we assume will last forever. We have a work ethic that causes us to labor even during our leisure. Health and circumstances, however, have a way of inserting some unexpected holidays. Disease can play havoc when our bodies are fatigued. The fast lane takes its toll on our emotional and spiritual stability. Suddenly we find ourselves sidelined simply because we refuse to take some time-outs.

Rest is not the only cure for our misuse of time. Worship can also heal our exhaustion. Taking time for God is taking time for ourselves. The Creator has a way of resuscitating His creatures. We are made to have fellowship with God, and to ignore it is to add spiritual fatigue to the weariness of our flesh.

To see God in the daily flow of things has a calming effect on all we do. It enables us to make the most of our time because God has equipped us for productivity. He frees us to find fulfillment within the parameters of our daily allotment of time. As the songwriter suggests, "Take time to be holy." Think on these things as you change your clock back this fall.

Walking with God

Walking with God is a beautiful way of describing our Christian pilgrimage. "A Closer Walk with God" is the essence of our daily journey with Him. Even though we struggle to make this a goal of our lives, we often fail to be where God desires. We find ourselves in the awkward position of walking more by ourselves than walking with God.

There are times in our walk with the Lord that we tend to walk ahead of Him. We become impatient with His slower pace and move on with what we assume is a better gait toward our goal. It is more like a race with God than a walk. We rush to conclusions. We hurry up our prayers. Rather than wait for clearer signals we compose our own agenda for the living of our days. In our haste to get where we are going we want God to quickly bless our plans. Walking ahead of God we tend to get exhausted. Because we do not wait upon the Lord we do not "mount up on wings as eagles." We do not run without getting weary and we grow faint in our walk. Like children who refuse to hold their parent's hand at a busy intersection we expose ourselves to much danger when we get ahead of God.

There are also times in our walk with God that we walk behind Him. We drag our feet. We lose interest in the things of God. Our affection becomes focused on things of the world. The church and our Christian witness become a burden rather than a lift. We take out our disappointment with people on God. When He does not fix every problem to our liking we withdraw. We do a little spiritual pouting. Even though we straggle far behind we want to keep Him in sight. We hear Him calling us onward and upward, but somehow the demands of a closer walk are too much. We give passive respect rather than passionate devotion in our walk with God.

Furthermore, there are times when in our walk with the Lord we walk all over Him. We trample His grace. We take advantage of His goodness. We expect Him to be merciful yet we are cruel. We expect Him to forgive our sins, but we refuse to forgive those who sin against us. We want the benefits of His blessings and His church without making a serious commitment to either. We want God, but we want Him on our own terms.

We stomp around Calvary and wonder why He does not come down from the cross and save us from the discomfort of having to identify with His death. Perhaps we want what God offers more than we want God.

Let us, therefore, not walk ahead of God. Let us not walk behind God. Neither let us walk all over God. Let us walk with God at the pace He chooses.

The Sabbath Principle

There is a Sabbath principle in life that must be observed if we are to be healthy and productive. It simply means that we cannot work nonstop without some time to recover our emotional and physical stamina. We cannot endure long periods of stress without some wholesome diversion.

Our human physique has many limitations, which requires periods of rest and relaxation. God made us this way. When He rested on the seventh day of creation, He punctuated the Sabbath principle for all His creatures. The fact that we have night and day, sunshine and rain, summer and winter reminds us that there is a time to work and a time to rest. This law of God is carved into the cycle of the seasons. How well have we learned it?

In our scientific world where nature no longer restricts our work, we tend to ignore the Sabbath principle. We fail to listen to the alarm system within our own weary bodies and, in so doing we bankrupt our souls before our years are spent. Insecurity and greed have sent us on an exhausting search for that pot of gold at the end of a very demanding rainbow. We are often overwhelmed by life's circumstances as stress takes its toll.

Yet, we are reluctant to find our rest in the Lord. God gave us the Sabbath principle, not to restrict us, but to restore us. God does not wish to inhibit our days of productivity. He wants to give our days a greater sense of fulfillment. Anxiety and fatigue will never allow us to be at our best. Overwork results in underachievement. Perhaps keeping a Sabbath day holy makes all our days holy unto the Lord.

On several occasions Jesus our Lord needed downtime and turned aside for uninterrupted moments with the Father. His human limitations left Him exhausted from dealing with the crowds. He taught His disciples and He is teaching us the need to stop what we are doing long enough to revive our mental, spiritual and physical energies.

It is a sin against our spirit and the spirit of God that lives within to destroy the house in which they dwell. Of course we are not equipped to live forever on this earth, but we are equipped to make the most of our years. In our mad rush to be materially secure, we must be still and know that He is God. In knowing Him we discover His Sabbath principle of rest for our work-weary lives. It is possible to find rest and recreation in the Lord.

Transcendence and Presence

Two words that are helpful in describing the nature of God's existence are transcendence and presence. The transcendence of God refers to that aspect of His being which is beyond us. It is the mystery and majesty of His being. The transcendence of God calls forth our worship and our praise. It causes us to stand in awe and reverent appreciation of all God is and has done. The transcendence of God gives meaning to the Lord's Day, the Lord's house, the Lord's work and the Lord's will. It is that which causes us to search for the deeper meaning of our own existence and relate to God as we would to no other person. The transcendence of God reminds us that there is no other like Him. He is holy other.

The presence of God, on the other hand, refers to His nearness. He who is great and distant and magnificent is also here and now. The special revelation of God in Jesus Christ helps us see the availability of God. If God can come to earth and dwell among us then He is not too far away to be concerned with our daily issues. God does not wish to be a distant deity unrelated to human affairs. His love brings Him into a personal relationship with anyone whose faith will allow it. The Holy Spirit is a constant, personal reminder that the God of the past and the future is also Lord of the present. He is beyond us, yet He is with us. He is creator, yet He is Savior. He is demanding, yet He is forgiving. He is God and we love Him.

How then do we grasp God's transcendence and presence? Perhaps we never fully comprehend it. We can celebrate, however, His depth and dignity in the way we worship. We can honor His presence through the practice of prayer. We can trust Him through humble obedience.

The Good Old Days

Sometimes we find ourselves wishing things could be the way they were. However, "the way they were" did not last very long. Whatever past circumstances we long for were temporary at best. Nostalgia is a fickle feeling. It can give us pleasant thoughts about days gone by and yet it can cause us to be so unrealistic about the past that we penalize our present and our future. Time moves on and change is inevitable. The "good old days" are but a memory of a time when we thought we had less stress and strain. We tend to forget the complications of life back then because present complications overshadow anything that ever has been. In an attempt to escape the painful perplexities of today we try to reconstruct yesterday according to how we wish it had been.

Even though things never were exactly the way we think they were, we must never stop making beautiful memories. It may be out of the way we think things were that we find the motivation to create a tomorrow in the way we want it to be. In this manner our memories are closely connected to our dreams. Perhaps the only way we can construct our dreams is by remembering the way we wish things had been.

Therefore, as we long for the "good old days", we can actually prepare ourselves for a better "new day" if we understand that every day has its share of hopes and horrors. The key is to be realistically aware that today we are making memories for the future. Yesterday is but a reminder that today contains the ingredients for a healthier tomorrow.

The major focus of our lives needs to be on the present. It is the only time we have. We cannot honestly reconstruct the past nor can we accurately produce the future. "Today is the day of salvation. Now is the accepted time." Forgiveness and grace as well as beautiful memories enable us to live with our past. The kind of hope that produces a positive attitude enables us to move graciously into the future. It is the disposition of the present moment that controls our appraisal of both.

Let us, therefore, never minimize this present breath of life, this existing heartbeat of love, and this moment of consciousness. Indeed the psalmist gave us great insight when he wrote, "This is the day the Lord has made. We will rejoice and be glad in it."

Being Alive

It is a wonderful thing to be alive, to be able to breathe, to see, to smell, and to touch. These things, which we take for granted, are vital to our health and wellbeing. God in His creative grace has chosen to share a bit of His existence with us and we call it life. He has given the energy of existence to all living things and we are blessed by it. The sights and sounds of life explode before us and we are often unaware of their presence. The laughter of children, the buzz of bees, chirping birds, trees, flowers, friendship and worship are just some of the things that give us a sense of awe and celebration to being alive. Sometimes the crises of life pungently bring to our attention those simple aspects of our daily routine, which have a marvelous capacity for our nurture.

Often in our search for the profound we miss the profundity of the simple. In our haste to show up at the important events of life we miss a thousand opportunities to allow little things to prepare us for big things. In our search for the significant we miss some of life's most pertinent pictures. Life has its own candid camera as well as its serious productions. It is a video victory when we have eyes to see and can really see. It is an audio miracle to have ears to hear and really hear.

Being alive is an event worth celebrating. The more we call attention to our aliveness the more grateful we are for being a part of God's existence. Every day we receive multiple blessings for being alive. Let us count them.

A Timely Prayer

It's a prayer for unity that we lift to you this day, O God. We pray for unity in our world where conflicting nations have chosen war as a means of settling their differences. Give those who precipitate such strife a reasonable spirit, so that hostile guns may once again be silent. May the principles of peace become more attractive than the weapons of war. May feeding and not fighting become the mission of productive nations.

We pray for unity in our country as opposing politicians seek to blame one another for our economic and social ailments. Give those in authority a responsible disposition toward the issues of our time. May they turn their mental energies toward solutions instead of accusations. May they give us reasons to be proud of the votes we cast. May "One Nation Under God" be the patriotic ambition of all Americans.

We pray for unity within all our Christian entities, as disunity is no respecter of institutions. Give those who have a following a sense of stewardship of their popularity. May they humbly and responsibly represent their denomination and the cause of Christ. Help us all to be cooperating Christians in a body of believers who understand that love will keep us strong. Although we may represent many lamps help us to stay committed to the true Light.

We pray for unity in our church where good people have a right to disagree agreeably. Help us to monitor our own feelings in keeping with the spirit of Jesus. Show us again and again that publicans, fishermen, zealots and a variety of folk can still commune at the Lord's holy table. Empower us to live and sing with gusto "Blest be the tie that binds our hearts in Christian love."

We make our pray in the Name of Him who calls us to take up our crosses and follow Him. Amen

Forward Through the Ages

There were strange and unusual rumblings in the religious community of that first century. It was not a stirring of the masses nearly as much as it was an excitement by a small minority of folk who allowed God in Christ to impact their lives. Rome had conquered the world and, in its conquest, had seemingly silenced the religious aspirations of most people. Whatever spiritual hopes there might have been were squelched under the heel of despotic tyranny.

Therefore, when a little band of folk nicknamed "Christians" emerged on the scene, they soon became the topic of religious conversation. The energy with which they worshiped and witnessed stood in contrast to the stale and anemic activities of traditional religions. The zeal with which they followed the Lord Christ caused government authorities to feel uneasy about their presence. Rome itself felt intimidated by a folk who preferred to say "Lord Christ" over "Lord Caesar."

In time, a people who took Jesus so seriously that they sold everything and gave everything was a threat to the political, economic, and religious structures of that day. Although Christians were loyal to government authority, they were suspect because of their greater loyalty to their Lord. Secular people, then and now, do not understand that a wholesome commitment to God is conducive to responsible citizenship. Government and God are not necessarily enemies. Only as government becomes god do Christians have a conflict of interest. A proper enthusiasm for Jesus is always law abiding if expressed in the context of a worthy input.

We learn today from those early Christians to be in the world but not of the world. We learn what it means to be salt as we seek to preserve that which will save us all. We learn to be light in a darkness that will often resent our need to shine. May the early churches' excitement be a role model for our churches today. What a difference it would make in our political and social rhetoric if indeed Jesus was Lord of our lives.

Peace with Our Past

Making peace with our past is essential to our spiritual health. On our journey through life we accumulate a lot of emotional baggage. The past tends to leave us with an assortment of mistakes, mistreatments, and missed opportunities. The accumulation of guilt, resentment, and fear can become a burden too heavy to carry at times. We come from imperfect backgrounds that have contributed to our own personal perplexities. Most of us have a lot to live up to and a lot to live down. Whatever our past has been we have to adjust to its realities. We cannot bury our heads in the sand and pretend it never existed. Our past is just as real as the present. Our inner child of the past is still with us. Yesterday's ledger affects today's balance sheet. We cannot fully escape where we have been, what we have done, and who has shared a part of our pilgrimage. Our past is like a boomerang. We cannot completely throw it away. It keeps coming back to influence our daily decisions and to affect our peace of mind.

In making peace with our past, honesty is our greatest ally. The ability to look back with integrity has many healthy implications. Because memory can play tricks on us, we can read more into a past occurrence than the truth can support. Memory can exaggerate or minimize whichever serves us best at the moment. As best we can, we need to let the past be the past and treat it with truth and grace. The pain of looking back occurs when there is an unwillingness to forgive and forget. In making peace with the past, not only do we forgive others but we forgive ourselves as well. We learn to let bygones be bygones as we move redemptively through the present into the future.

Whenever we make peace with our past, it will be a spiritual experience. Faith is a prerequisite, repentance is a necessity, and grace makes it happen. The truth of the matter is that in Christ we can experience peace about our past. Dysfunctional relationships can be healed in the light of His forgiving love. Mistreatment, rejection and lifelong anxieties can be resolved when we are serious about making peace with our past. Perhaps Paul said it best when he wrote. "But one thing I do, forgetting what is

Growing Through Risk

Most of us spend much time and energy looking for a sure thing. We try to live our lives with as little risk as possible. It would be great if life came with a solid guarantee that nothing unpredictable would arise. What if any chance of ever losing our job was all removed? What if all our investments were guaranteed a maximum return? What if a school made certain every student could earn perfect grades? What if a marriage contract could be written to eliminate every element of risk? What if a church could assure its members all their needs would be met and all their questions resolved? What if God suddenly offered guaranteed results for all our efforts?

We could go on "what if-ing" for a long time, but life is not put together that way. The faith factor has to be considered in everything we do. Life is risky business. We take a chance every day we live. Faith is our greatest asset because it helps to relieve the tension of total risk. It causes us to see that God is love and all things work together for good if we love Him. Faith allows us to see beyond the immediate circumstances to future possibilities.

We do not stick our heads in the sand and ignore life's difficulties. We accept risk as a legitimate aspect of human life. At times we are hurt by it, yet we learn from it. It stimulates our fear, yet it cultivates our trust. God is never nearer than when we look up through the dark pit of our despair to see the bright light of His love.

As long as we live, risk will never be eliminated, but it can be creatively anticipated. By faith, we can live on the "tiptoe" of expectancy, where every new emergency is an adventure with God. This does not presume a life of "fairytale-ism." Hard knocks will come and sometimes their blows will be difficult to absorb. The Chinese word for "crisis" has two characters. One means danger. The other means opportunity. Perhaps there is a lesson here. Risk may mean danger, but it can also be an opportunity to grow.

If risk overwhelms us we cannot live by faith. When this occurs we lose a sense of stewardship about life. We are reluctant to invest ourselves in anything worthwhile unless the returns are obvious. We cannot depart with our tithes and offerings lest our security be threatened. Fear settles in, as we prefer a more predictable way of life. Our strength, however, comes from making peace with risk. It is here we find the courage to keep on keeping on.

Life is always at some turning point. We must make sure that the point around which it is turning is God. In growing through risk we learn to trust a stable God.

"Been There, Done That"

The statement is often made, "Been there, done that." It is a catchy cliché to express a lack of interest in repeating an unfavorable event. In some ways it is a sad saying. It sounds like a bit of life has had an unpleasant effect upon us. We do not wish to relive an experience that has left us less than enthusiastic about it. We tend to rebel against going through another episode of undesirable circumstances. Some places we go and some things we do are relatively pleasant at the time, but lack the interest for us to do them again. "Been there, done that" is sad if it expresses a mild indifference to life. Much of life is repetition. It is not composed entirely of unrepeatable performances. We go on the same stage and play the same role day after day. Life is a series of having "been there, done that" over and over again.

Since we cannot escape many of life's repeatable circumstances, we must learn to grow through them. In fact, we can learn to appreciate the beautiful consistencies of life. Our survival depends on the fact that some things occur with predictable frequency. We eat, we drink, we work, we play, we laugh, we cry, we hurt, we heal, we sleep, and we wake. These and many more recurring circumstances are necessary for our existence. At times they may seem monotonous, but in the long run we are energized by life's routines.

Of course, everything that happens to us and within us is not pleasant. There is a part of life's journey we do not wish to re-travel. As we wisely interpret both the bitter and the sweet, we can learn to put most things in proper perspective. Having "been there, done that" can equip us to go to wherever life takes us and do whatever needs to be done. Experience is the best teacher, even though some experiences are not looked upon with favor. We cannot always pick and choose life's event, but we can choose to make the most of them.

Unless life teaches us something, "been there, done that" is only an expression in useless futility. Therefore, let us "go there, do that" and grow beyond whatever disappointments occur. Perhaps we need to revise our cliché to say, "Been there, done that and grown through it." God can use what we have survived to help others survive. He calls us to comfort and encourage others by the comfort and encouragement we have received. We do not live in a perfect paradise. We live in the kind of world, which requires us to be keepers and caretakers of one another. Whatever we lose, others can help us find. Whatever we gain, others can help us enjoy. Life can be full of as much fulfillment as we are willing to find when we have "been there, done that."

Busy Boredom

The tedious turmoil of our times keeps us in a state of distraction. We never seem to find the satisfying fulfillment for which we dream. A busy boredom causes us to lose the excitement of what we do. We run here and there searching for the meaning of life and wonder why we never find it. We wait for some tremendous revelation that will clarify the issues of our lives. We pray for some spectacular event to awaken our drowsy spirits. Life passes by so quickly we study it only in the past tense. The present offers little time to explore its vast opportunities. Here we are caught in mid-passage waiting for the future, yet unable to learn from the past. At best we are pilgrims on a journey, wondering if our excursion will falter before the end.

Perhaps we try too hard to have a meaningful existence. We push to make things happen that never will nor never should. For the most part, life is what goes on while we are waiting for something to happen. There is a sense in which we must learn to let things happen in the context of God's holy will. We cannot always program our lives into neat little packages of rigid predictability. As Jesus told Nicodemus, "the wind blows where it will." There is a sense of mystery to our lives in Christ. The freshness of a new thing keeps the challenge ever before us. Not knowing everything gives us excitement and anticipation. Let us, therefore, not fear the ultimate questions whose answers seem to elude us. Sometimes we have to do the best we know and then find the will of God in looking back. Of course, hindsight is twenty-twenty vision, but at least it is vision. It is a confidence builder to know God has been with us even if it is an insight, which comes after the fact.

The Lord God of everything and everywhere and everybody does not wish to tantalize us with the unknown. He wants us to grow into the unknown with the kind of faith, which calls us to our daily task. It is like the blind man healed by Jesus. He was interrogated by the religious leaders. His simple response was, "This one thing I know, whereas I was blind, now I see." He did not grasp the "hows" and "whys." He simply celebrated what he had experienced. Life is surely happening while we wait for it to happen. Let us celebrate our "aliveness" even in our ignorance as we allow the truth to set us free from our busy boredom.

Growing Old with Grace

The poet made a healthy observation when he wrote, "Let me grow lovely growing old." He understood that life can become either bitter or better as our year's advance. We are created with a capacity to adjust to whatever circumstances life imposes upon us. If we develop a positive disposition toward negative situations we can find the poet's beauty in growing old. On the other hand, if we allow negativity to dominate we will develop a sour disposition. The years will take a terrible toll if we allow circumstances to defeat us. The poet implies that it is possible to have an aging attractiveness. We can turn the scars of life into beauty marks. Our wrinkles can produce a smile instead of a frown. Our experiences can be used as a tender tool to encourage the next generation. As the years transpire, we can develop the gift of growing old.

It is important that we monitor the aging process in our lives to see what is happening. Sometimes it is helpful to make a comparative study of those who precede us. Some folk remain vivacious and kind to the end of their days. Others become disgruntled and hateful in their twilight years. They develop frowns on their faces. They appear angry and sad. We do well to work on our faces, not so much with cosmetics, but with some smiles and laughter that let our inner beauty show through. Expressions on our faces reveal a lot about us. It might surprise us to know what others think about our countenance. Does our appearance reflect the joy of life or the sadness of growing old?

The kind of person we are has a way of emerging to the surface. Character cannot be camouflaged indefinitely. Our true person comes to the surface by how we look, what we say, and how we say it. The attention we give to our soul's development adds more to our beauty than any kind of facelift. If we want our cosmetics to really work, then we add some love, joy, peace, and hope to our outward appearance. Personal radiance is the product of good grooming and personal hygiene from the inside out.

How well do you smile? Do you reflect God's love or the devil's

What are We Dying for?

When we reflect upon the cross of Jesus, we are impressed by the fact that He invites us to share death with Him. In following Him we expose ourselves to a cross-like life. His promise is that in losing our lives we will find our lives. Love has no greater expression than laying down one's life for another.

The gospel is a cause worth dying for and many martyrs have made the ultimate sacrifice. The Christian life is a risk-taking adventure. We cannot escape its call to death even as it offers the highest quality of life. Because life is our most precious asset we cannot make a total commitment until it too has been offered. We can never overestimate the power of dying love.

There is a sense in which we are all dying for something. Some folk are dying for cigarettes. They are smoking themselves into the throes of lung cancer. There are those dying for excessive use of narcotics. They are drinking themselves toward alcoholism and cirrhosis. They are popping pills with fatal implications. Some people are dying for their careers. They are exhausting themselves into workaholics. They are losing the joy of their work in the addiction to work. We are beginning to see more and more people dying for food. Poor diets and gluttonous eating habits are creating serious health problems. There is any number of people dying for attention. They worry so much about being neglected it eats away at their nervous system. Yes, in one way or another we are all dying for something.

The big question, which confronts us, is this: Is what we are dying for worth dying for? This is where the gospel comes to our rescue and offers us something bigger than ourselves to which we can be committed. Giving ourselves away to worthy causes is what the Christian life is all about. From the time we are born we begin the process of death. Hopefully on the journey we can find a life worth living through the things worth dying for. Some people are dying for no good reason. Other people are dying with a peace and a purpose from God.

The cross of our Lord Jesus becomes our model for both living and dying. The spirit of sacrifice is necessary for abundant living and peaceful dying. Our Lord taught us that unless a seed falls into the ground and dies it cannot produce life. Dying daily to ourselves we are resurrected in fulfillment. Giving ourselves away to that which is high and holy exposes us to that which is high and holy. May the Lord God of the cross give us a cross-bearing witness in a world, which still crucifies innocence. Since we are going to die at some time, let us make it worthwhile.

Death in Gospel Perspective

In the evening of life there is a sunset glow. The culmination of faith focuses upon the light at the end of the tunnel. Belief in the hereafter guards against the clouds of gloom. When there is little left but God and the human soul, the cares of life lose their ability to harass us. The pains of the past are absorbed in tomorrow's hope. People who seek to do us harm have no power to interrupt our fellowship with God. We lose our fear of those who can only harm the body. We gain our courage from Him who is the lover and protector of our souls. Twilight time is a peaceful interlude between life's rigorous demands and heaven's quiet repose. The closer we get to God the more we find the joy of somber thoughts in the expression of our praise.

For some it may seem strange to reflect upon the final chapters of life. Death seems so far away when we are young. Why focus on that morbid reality before our days are half spent? Should not the energy of youth be spent on things at hand? The answer is most assuredly "yes." To become unnecessarily preoccupied with the end of life before life has hardly begun could lead to a premature despair. However, were it not for death we might never learn the meaning of life. The fact that one day we shall die motivates us to make the most of our days. Deep within us is a need to contribute something worthwhile before the final curtain falls.

Another reason for us to reflect on death is that we prepare for its impact upon our lives. There is no way we are going to get out of this world alive. Coming to terms with death is much better than rebelling against it. The final chapter can be one of tragedy or triumph, whichever we prefer. Faith in God leads us to believe there is more than a traumatic conclusion to life. There can be creative anticipation of what lies ahead. Death can be seen as friend and not foe. We do not have to go on living with the limitations, penalties, and perplexities of this life. We can move into that "mysterious realm like one who wraps the drapery of his couch about him and lies down to pleasant dreams."

"Come, then, let us reason together. Though your sins be as scarlet, they shall be white as snow." Though your life be filled with misery and woe, it shall be as bright as God's promises. You may feel no need to think about death. In doing so, however, you may find a death-defying disposition toward the rest of life. May the evening of life give you a sunset glow.

Death Defying Faith

How does one die who never prays nor talks to God about anything? How does one approach death when there has been no effort to claim God's death defying promises? Surely it must be a shock to one's spiritual system to face the unknown with an unknown God. The trauma of death is too much for our human resources alone. The thoughts of dying require us to have some serious thoughts about God. Our fragile understanding of our departure from this life is proof that we need more than the human intellect to guide us into eternity.

We are not equipped to face death with calloused indifference and that too is a part of God's grace. He requires us to have sober thoughts about our eternal destiny and then offers us a place He has gone to prepare. He frightens us with the prospects of entering the darkness all alone and then He promises to be with us always. He lures us to the edge of life with resurrection hope and bids us come unto Him and find rest.

Our hope is a matter of faith and acceptance. He does not force His house of "many mansions" upon us. He does not walk beside us as an uninvited presence. It is a simple gospel of receiving what Jesus has to offer and we complicate it greatly when we try to earn it. Heaven is a gift we do not deserve; therefore, dying as well as living are a matter of grace.

Only with Christ can we face death with the assurance that God who called us into life has something special for us in death. Who knows what we might grow to become in the hereafter.

Biblical Perspectives

Finding Our Song

The meaning of music has a profound effect upon our spiritual dispositions. The gospel in song has a way of touching the depth of our emotions and at times bringing forth both tears and smiles. The capacity of our souls to burst forth in melody is undoubtedly one of God's greatest gifts. The release of our emotions in music offers healing and relief for our sin weary lives. The most hopeful truth of the ages is that God gives a reason to sing.

Amid the disharmony and discord of evil's tragic domain there is the song of salvation. We worship a God who not only saves, but a God who calls us to celebrate that fact with vocal praise. In singing we have an opportunity to say things to God and about God that we can say in no other way. Music gives expression to our soul's deepest desire for inner harmony. Even as we sing God is singing over us.

Although we are not all gifted with the ability to sing or play a musical instrument, we are all equipped to respond to the music of life. The heart's true song is more than instruments, notes and noise. It is a melody of our being which rises from the great convictions of our souls. It is a harmony with God and God's purposes in our world. It is the music which flows, when through confession and commitment, Jesus is made Lord of life. It is the song of salvation simply expressing the overflowing joy of God's forgiveness.

How blessed we are when the music of our lips and our instruments are inspired by the deeper song of our souls. Worship occurs, either private or public, when our deep inner singing begins. It is a musical heart which finds joy in the Lord.

Therefore, let us join the Psalmist and "Sing unto the Lord, praise His name and proclaim His salvation day after day." The Bible admonishes us to "Make a joyful noise unto the Lord all you lands." Our daily peace of mind and soul will depend upon our ability to find our song.

Secrets

Secrets often come in a variety of packages. Some secrets are designed to surprise. Certain facts are concealed in order to startle the recipient of a gift. Battle plans are hidden from the enemy to launch a surprise attack. The element of surprise is always dependent on secrecy. Another set of secrets is designed to protect our privacy. What is everybody's business is nobody's business. Because we live in a world where unscrupulous folk would take advantage of us, we cannot go public with our financial affairs or with our personal business. Secrets about our private fears and idiosyncrasies protect us from embarrassing comments by insensitive people.

We withhold certain internal information because there is a private aspect to our being. We have a personal relationship with ourselves containing things only God needs to know. Because we are private as well as public creatures we will always have secrets. This does not imply that all our secrets are bad. It means that we have a right to keep some things to ourselves.

Secrets, however, have a way of seeping through our most sophisticated concealment. For one thing, certain people are always prying into who we are. They make it a point to investigate and analyze everything we do and say. They pose as friends, but in reality they are searching for the cracks in our armor. Once they find them our secrets are exposed.

In another sense there are people with whom we think we can confide. We bear our souls to such friends with many of our well-kept secrets. That person then bears "our soul" to someone else considered confidential, and before long our private life is the topic of public discussion. When this occurs we have a tendency to withdraw and bear our souls to no one. We turn inward wondering if there is anyone we can trust.

At best secrets are fragile. We do not live in a confidential world. Sinful folk are always looking for someone weaker than themselves. Inferior people are always looking for someone more inferior. Gossip is a thrilling pastime for people who enjoy sharing our secrets or anyone's secrets, for that matter. It is a game some people play trying to make their conversation more shocking and provocative to their audience.

How, then, do we protect our secrets? In one way it would be well not to have some secrets. Sin can cause secrets. Unresolved guilt makes us cling to them. Perhaps we protect our own secrets of human frailty by protecting others with similar secrets. "Judge not that you be not judged" is applicable because "we have all sinned and come short of the glory of God."

Confidential people will most likely be treated confidentially. We tend to reap the seeds of gossip that we sow. "For with what judgment you judge you shall likewise be judged."

Reflecting God's Love

The unconditional love of God is our best example of how we ought to relate to one another. There is an acceptance as well as a freedom in the expression of God's affection toward us. He stands at the door of our lives knocking and waiting. He does not crash in the door to take us by force. He does not harass us with the automatic weapons of a coercive legalism. By gentle cords, He leads us into the "green pastures and beside the still waters" of holy fellowship.

By no means does He condone our awkward behavior, nor does He tolerate our sinister spirits. Yet, in the context of grace, He allows us room to repent as we find the courage to confess. He accepts us for who we are and journeys with us on the pilgrimage of spiritual growth. He does not expect the impossible, nor does He minimize our highest potential. He is God, He is good and "His kindness endures to all generations."

What a difference it would make if we could learn from God how to reflect the essence of His grace. Even though we are not good ourselves, we often require an impossible perfection from others. We nose around in other people's lives trying to find a reason to feel superior. We find it difficult to believe in others because we do not believe in ourselves. If, somehow, we could live out of grace instead of judgment, we would no longer feel the exhausting need to conquer and intimidate in the name of the Lord.

Life is a lot like a storm where the goal is rescue and not ridicule. We are all bound for the "Promised Land," but the wilderness travel requires a lot of love. The discipline of thoughts, words, and behavior keeps us close to the mind of Christ. A Servant spirit will keep us saying and doing the things, which create a sense of fellowship to life. Our most practical prayer for good relations with others may be, "Let the words of my mouth and the meditations of my heart be acceptable in Thy sight, O Lord, my strength and my Redeemer."

Listening Ears

Communication is one of life's most necessary events. The ability to convey our thoughts to another person and to receive their thoughts as well is indeed a blessing. Words, whether written or spoken, become the vehicle by which we express what is on our minds.

Words beautifully arranged in perfect composition or in eloquent speech, however, do not necessarily mean communication has occurred. We may write or say what we really mean, but unless the one reading or listening is on the same frequency we may not accurately communicate. Words sometimes fail us because of the human tendency to misunderstand. How frustrating when our best attempts to communicate are misinterpreted. Good communication occurs when we work hard at giving and receiving the same signals.

It is not always other people's fault when they misunderstand what we think is clear speech. We may need to sit where they sit and listen with their ears to what we are saying. Seeking to understand another's misunderstanding is one of life's most loving expressions. We all have an emotional as well as a mental vocabulary. Some words have an emotional meaning, which is not found in the dictionary. The cultural and psychological circumstances, which birthed us, have a lot to do with what we hear and what we say. To grasp this reality is an aid to good communication.

Sometimes we hear only what we want to hear. Our thought processes are so slanted we find it difficult to be objective in our listening. When this happens it is easy to quote someone out of context. We express the opinion of others from the perspective of our own opinion. Such mishandling of another's conversation greatly hinders communication. It gives the appearance of dishonesty even though we simply repeat what we thought we heard.

Jesus understood the human defects of speech and hearing. On one occasion He said, "Let your 'yea' be 'yea' and your 'nay' be 'nay.'" In other

When we speak and listen in love, good communication will often be the end result. May the words of our mouths and the listening of our ears be acceptable in His sight.

Gospel Economics

Financial stewardship is the backbone of the Christian enterprise. There can be no profound sharing of one's life in Christ unless it includes a monetary commitment. The Lord God of our prosperity has required us to be faithful in using that with which He has entrusted us. We cannot escape the awesome assignment of financing our part of God's involvement in ministry and witness. The economics of the gospel is a fascinating journey in faith and loyalty. It is unbelievable what God can do when our financial stewardship is equal to our godly dreams. The call of God is not only to witness and work but to give as well. The tithe is not just a guideline for giving, it is a principle written into the structure of our being. It was God's design from the beginning that we recognize His ownership of all things by returning the tithe.

The principle of sacrifice is at the heart of what it means to belong to God. In fact, our witness and our work are of little consequence if they are not supported by a strong financial commitment. If we yield everything to God but our money, we will soon lose the fervor of our faith. The gospel is a risk-taking venture. Our proclamation is hollow if it is not backed up by a risk-taking commitment. Faith will wither and die if we do not invest in that which we believe. Our most tangible investment, which gives credence to our testimony, is the tithe. The principle of giving is instilled in the universe. No matter how much we give, we cannot out give God. We learn, therefore, from a love-giving God that the best things in life are not free.

God so loved the world that He has invited us to join the Christian enterprise with our tithes and offerings. In fact, we lose respect and love for ourselves when we let others do our serving and our giving. A deadbeat Christian is no better than a person who expects a free ride from welfare with no intention of working even though he or she may be able. There is a warm sense of satisfaction when the offering plate is passed and we have done our part. We are not saved from our sins by what we give, but we are saved from the sin of being ungrateful stewards. Tithing is God's plan for growing Christians and that is the basis of

Prejudice

Prejudice is a strange and powerful aspect of human ignorance. It has thousands of cunning ways to create unbelievable barriers. It thrives on the lack of information. It grows in the midst of suspicion and innuendoes. Prejudice does not need facts to give impetus to its horrid influence. It is propelled by the false winds of irresponsible conversation. It holds us in the grip of an unbending legalism.

It is mostly out of fear that we suspect those who are not our kind. We do not wait for truth when we want to believe the worst about those whom we dislike. Prejudice keeps us in the dark even when the light of other people's opinions is before us. It is difficult for us to see beyond the color of skin, language barriers and any number of objectionable characteristics. Truth that comes in an unfamiliar package is unacceptable. Like Pharisees of old we cannot accept a Messiah who is different.

Even though we wish it were not so, we are all quite gullible to the Satanic devices of prejudice. We are forever looking for those folk toward whom we can feel superior. We cling tenaciously to those ideas and customs, which give us security of thought and keep our traditions intact. People and ideas, which challenge us to think "outside the box", are found to be objectionable. We simply cannot tolerate that which is different.

Religion is a most vulnerable prey of prejudice. Jesus found it that way in His day and strongly rebuked the religious leaders for their narrow opinions. He sought to redeem His people from established habit and give them the truth, which would make them free. The mind of Christ is our only hope against the power of prejudice. His gospel is good news to everyone who is victimized by an unbending disposition. His grace can paralyze our prejudice

Economic Security

Whether we admit it or not, economic security is vital to our sense of wellbeing. It affects the way we think and act in more ways than one. Many of life's major decisions are based on the economic factor. Our behavior is often the result of materialistic influences. Of course, economic security for one person is not the same for another. We all have different levels of financial satisfaction. We are all caught in the grip of our own monetary needs as we struggle to make the most of our material resources.

Because money is an important item in the structure of human affairs, we do well to analyze its emotional and spiritual impact upon us. For most of us, money represents the highest expression of material security. It offers not only the necessities of life but the luxuries, which seem to be more needful in our affluent society.

The Biblical mandate does not minimize the meaning of money in our lives. It seeks to attract the powerful potential of our financial resources for the glory of God. What we do with our money is an index to what we consider most important. It is not wrong to have money and the things money can buy. It is wrong when our whole sense of wellbeing is unduly affected by what we have or do not have. We must not allow our scale of values in life to give an exaggerated priority to the moneymaking apparatus. Our true worth is not determined by what we have but by who we are. A sense of material well-being is as much spiritual as it is financial.

Extravagant living is always nervous about not having enough. When greed rather than need is our goal, we will never know the peace of economic contentment. Somewhere in the context of our faith in God we must accept our financial boundaries. Living beyond our means is a sin against reality. We penalize ourselves emotionally and spiritually when we have nothing left to share. As Christians, money can have a marvelous ministry in our lives. We are happiest and most secure economically when we learn to trust God and use our money in ways

Who Then Is Holy?

Do you think God has given us His holy inspired Word to be a vehicle for debate? Is He pleased when people fuss about who believes it the best or the most? Did He inspire the adjectives and code words, which have segregated people into competing camps of spiritual argumentations? Is holy Word and holy living separate entities? No! No! Surely not.

Do you think God sent His virgin born Son into the world so that we might entertain ourselves with theories of how it happened? Is He really honored when that night of miracles becomes nothing more to us than another way to judge the validity of one's faith? Is heaven's nativity chorus blasphemed by our pleasing platitudes and our hollow worship? Has evil captured one of Christianity's most holy days? No! No! Surely not.

Do you think our Lord performed miracles of healing, signs and wonders simply to create a climate of controversy? Was Jesus only a divine magician who performed tricks to get people's attention? Was resurrection from death designed only to inspire theological discussion? No! No! Surely not.

Did the Holy Spirit come to focus our attention on tongues, fire, and super emotionalism? Does He give us gifts so that we might win spiritual popularity contests? Does He enjoy the religious statistical games we play? Does God really empower us to exert our superiority over people struggling with their sins? No! No! Surely not.

Did He give us the book of Revelation so that we might argue eschatology (Study of end times)? Are mystery and symbolism and "last things" the only gospel we have? Is the unfolding of the ages merely a puzzle to exercise human minds or does God have a loving purpose? Did He give us the church merely as a pit in which to hiss at one another? Does our Lord get pleasure in watching us feud about who is greatest in the kingdom? No! No! Surely not.

Well, then, woe to us if we misuse God's resources. Woe to us if we become mere judges of people rather than compassionate lovers of souls. Surely, surely we all know who it is who would divert our attention from the content to the container. How clever of the devil to make us religious rather than righteous. Surely we must decide which is more important.

Who then is holy? God be merciful to all us sinners struggling in God's birth canal to be born again. No one and again I say "no one" of us can look down our spiritual noses at another as though we were more holy. By grace we are all being saved. Amen

Keepership

The story of the first family as recorded in Genesis has a sad scenario. Cain killed his brother Abel. Afterward God came to Cain inquiring about the whereabouts of Abel. Cain's response was a sarcastic question. "How do I know? Am I my brother's keeper?" God's reaction and punishment of Cain strongly impressed upon him that he was indeed his brother's keeper. The story becomes a kind of parable instructing us as to our responsibility toward one another. God does not permit us to take another life nor treat another life with disrespect. Reverence for human life and our watch-care over it is the essential lesson we get from this ancient tragedy.

Throughout the scriptures we sense a call to "keepership" to which we do well to adhere. We cannot neglect a fellow human being with an easy conscience. We are made equally interdependent and our Source of creation makes us accountable to one another. We cannot plead ignorance as though we did not know life's stewardship included our brother. The most ancient Decalogue reviews the many ways we are to care for one another. We keep the commandments by keeping each other. Neglecting another person's need is a form of Biblical heresy just as killing the spirit is another form of murder. If we do not look out for our brother, then sooner or later his pain becomes our pain and his hunger becomes our source of starvation.

Our "keepership" does not mean we hover over our neighbor making sure he or she is our kind of Christian. It is not a matter of judging others by making sure they are worthy of whatever attention and care we may give them. Jesus reached out to the unclean leper as well as the neatly dressed bureaucrat. He offered grace to those of ill repute and corrected those who thought they knew it all. He taught us the meaning of our "keepership" in both word and deed. Who would have thought that dying love was an example for all of us to follow? We cannot eliminate our brother without our Lord inquiring as to his whereabouts. We had better keep up with one another lest we be kept from the kingdom.

God's Ways

God has a way to do everything that needs to be done. His power is magnificent. His wisdom is significant. His love is patient and His grace is sufficient. God's ways are not our ways, but the mystery of His work does not diminish His ability to perform. God has a way to reach the sinner for whom we pray and the sinner who says a prayer.

He has a way to reconcile the hostile neighbor even as He creates a climate of forgiveness. God has a way to prepare rest for the weary even as He inspires the lazy. He has a way to love the lost even as He rebukes the redeemed. God has a way to get glory from the insignificant even as He humbles the proud.

God has a way to heal the brokenhearted even as He softens the hard-hearted. He has a way to turn defeat into victory and to make tears the product of a joyous heart. God has a way to save you to the uttermost if your faith will allow you to trust His word. He has a way to bring you peace even as His truth cuts like a two-edged sword. God has a way to perform miracles if our eyes are conditioned to see. Yes, God has a way and perhaps Jesus said it best. "I am the way, the truth and the life. No man cometh unto the Father but by me."

The human tendency, however, is to do it our way. There seems to be within us an inherent pride that often hinders the godly process. Deep down we know that God has a way, and we know it is best, but somehow we mismanage our options. We often seek revenge rather than turn the other cheek. We run ahead rather than wait upon the Lord to renew our strength. We walk through the valleys of pain, disease, and death as though we could do it on our own. There is a vast sea of human need around us, but we are often islands of unconcern. Rather than go, we stay. Rather than serve, we sit. We want the peace that passes all understanding without the pain of the cross. We say, "Lord, Lord," but we do not do the Father's will. We want God, but we want Him on our own terms. Perhaps our greatest hope is in the fact that God has ways to teach us that His ways are best. Our greatest response is "Here I am

The Beatitudes

My spirit was broken. There was absolutely nothing good about me. I felt miserable and alone. Then I heard Him say, "Blessed are the poor in spirit for theirs is the kingdom of heaven." What joy to my troubled soul.

I grieved and fretted in my pain, yet He insisted that all who mourn would be comforted. It brought solace to my soul to know that He was present in my inner agony. He was aware that I suffered grief.

In reality I wanted to be somebody big. I had strength and I wanted to exert my power. In caution His words were clear, "Blessed are the meek for they shall inherit the earth." Only in humility can there be real power.

There was still something missing. I had a longing to understand the particulars of my being. There was a drought in my soul for something higher and better. In love He assured me that I was blessed to hunger and thirst for righteousness and I would be filled. My appetite for goodness would be satisfied.

I loved people and I wanted them to love me in return. I did not want to hurt anyone nor be hurt by them. It was helpful to hear "Blessed are the merciful for they shall obtain mercy." In other words, I would receive as I had given.

My questions about God came fast and furious. I wanted to know more. I wanted to know Him. "How does it happen?" I asked. It is a purity of heart that enabled me to see God. Pure motives lead to better understanding and greater vision.

Not only did I want to know and understand more about God, I wanted to reflect His character. I wanted to please Him in my daily life. If He were truly my Father, then I wanted to act like His child. It was a powerful revelation to hear Him say, "Blessed are the peacemakers for they shall be called the children of God." In promoting peace, I would best resemble my Father.

Yet, when I did my best, people were critical and hurtful toward me. I could not understand folk rejecting my loving efforts to be a servant. "Why is it, Lord?" I asked. He did not explain why, but He called me blessed and told me to rejoice for I had great reward in heaven. And that was enough for me.

Religious Intimidation

Intimidation is a terrible curse on the human scene. It crushes folk who allow the overbearing prominence of others to take away their self-esteem. Certain people never achieve their spiritual potential because they are intimidated by those who seem superior. Intimidation is a tool we use on one another to win arguments and to chastise those in disagreement with us. It is not a comfortable attitude for either the intimidator or the intimidated. The intimidator does not really prove a point. He or she merely embarrasses folk into submission. The intimidated are not really humble. They are simply humiliated.

So often in church intimidation is a tool for teaching and preaching. For example, here is a preacher who presents a beautiful truth, which is quite capable of being received as presented. Yet, he chooses to punctuate his point with the intimidating statement that "if you do not see it this way then you do not know the God I know." Have you ever heard someone say in disagreement to some thought "that is not the way my Bible reads?" Such statements are subtle attempts to use "my God" and "my Bible" to intimidate others toward belief.

The truth of the matter is that intimidation is never an effective means of witness. The gospel of grace is quite capable of doing its own convicting without human coercion. The bottom line is that we have all been created in the image of God to find our self-worth in Him and to help others find their worth there also. Only in Him can we find relief from the curse of intimidation.

A Father's Lament

"O my son, Absalom, my son, Absalom. If only I had died instead of you, O Absalom, my son, Absalom." How did you grow up to be such a rebel? Why did you have such hatred for me and the kingdom I serve? Are you a product of my own household? I know I am much to blame. If only I had been a better father, you would not now be my enemy. If only I had nurtured you in your youth and trained you as a young man, I would not now be in the deepest grief of my life. I set a bad example before you and for that reason, you have just cause to hate me.

My time was spent on the affairs of my country rather than the encouragement of my sons. I was much more interested in conquest than in the concerns of my family. I thought the enemy was out there. Little did I know he was growing up in my household, eating from my table and becoming more bitter every day.

O, Absalom, it is I who should have died because it was my blunders, which broke the bond between you and me. If only I had died, I could now be free of the accumulated guilt of a faithless father. Please forgive me, Absalom. As a young father, I did not think anything was more important than my career. I thought I was pleasing God by being a conscientious king. I thought my family would be proud of me if I were a big success.

O, Absalom, you are more precious than all the kingdoms I have conquered. If only I had reared you properly, you would have made a magnificent king. You had such charisma and charm. People would have followed you to the ends of the earth. Now that you are gone, I have nothing but regret. If only I could reverse the calendar and call back the time when your childish attitude was in my power to mold.

I know it cannot be, but perhaps someone will learn from me. Perhaps some father will sense the intensity of my pain and turn from the ways of an over-demanding culture to a call toward responsible fatherhood. Maybe some men will put success in its proper perspective and stop to smell the roses of family involvement along the way.

"Have mercy on me, O God, according to your unfailing love. Wash away all my iniquity and cleanse me from my sin. Against you have I sinned and lost a son in the process."

Inner Music

As David composed his prayer of confession in Psalm Fifty-One, he alluded to the fact that he had lost his song. The sin of his life had taken the sweet music from his lips and the melody from his heart. The greatest pain of this period of spiritual digression was his songless heart. The joy of his salvation had been put on hold. He longed for a clean heart and a steadfast spirit so that his testimony could once again be authentic. He wanted to sing aloud of God's righteousness and show forth praise unto his God.

Have you ever lost your song? Has sin separated you from the divine keyboard? Has indifference caused you to lose the will to sing? It happens sometimes and when it does it is a joyless existence. Your inner music is necessary for your peace and composure. The Biblical concept of joy is often accompanied by singing.

Life was made for music; not that we are all gifted performers, but there is joy and there is rhythm and there is laughter and there is excitement in God's design for each of us. And that is music. Life is not so much a solo as it is an orchestra or a choir. We blend our individual instruments and talents into the melody of life. We may be many but we are one in the Spirit and that too is music. Happy is the person who finds real harmony in commitment and love.

When we lose our zest for life, we lose our song. When this happens our only hope is in Him who first taught us to sing. If we let Him, He will teach us the songs of confession, repentance and faith. With our human commitment He will compose a ministry of music from every detail of our lives. Then we can say with the Psalmist, "My tongue will joyfully sing of thy righteousness."

Coloring Outside the Lines

The phrase "coloring outside the lines" refers to the actions and disposition of folk who do not always function within the confines of that which is generally accepted. These persons are not inhibited by majority opinion. They are not controlled by what everyone else wishes them to think and do. They have a mind of their own. For the most part these are the people who give us new inventions. They challenge the way things have always been, offering us new ways of facing old problems. Creativity abounds when there is a willingness to "color outside the lines." Sometimes the unusual and the unexpected can shock us out of the way things have always been to the way they can be better. As a society we are indebted to individuals and groups who have had the courage to challenge the status quo by offering a more hopeful and helpful way.

On the other hand, "coloring outside the lines" can be disastrous. Changing everything does not necessarily represent a better way. People who are different just for the sake of being different are not always different for the right reasons. Some folk who "color outside the lines" are obnoxious and difficult while others are vain and vulgar. There are some things that are tried and true for the centuries. Our world has some absolutes from which we deviate at our own peril. We do not experiment with moral and ethical behavior. We cannot produce a better society by total replacement. We build upon sound structures by changing only that which has served its effectiveness or that which tends to demoralize and destroy. It is wrong to treat an ingrown toenail by amputating the leg.

In many ways Jesus "colored outside the lines." He "colored outside the lines" in terms of outmoded religious customs. He dealt differently with sinners, Samaritans, women, and other folk of lesser standing. Jesus "colored outside the lines" when it came to such things as love, forgiveness, prayer, worship, sacrifice, and grace. He was not a conventional Rabbi nor was He an acceptable prophet in most people's eyes. Yet, He did not come to destroy the Law or the Prophets but to fulfill them. Let us, therefore, be courageous enough to "color outside

Growing Through Adversity

Deep within the valley of despair, we are often conditioned to find the green pastures of spiritual nourishment and the still waters of God's grace. Perhaps we are never nearer God than when our hearts are heavy and our mental resources seem exhausted. Too often, in the proud world of our own achievements, we develop an arrogance, which denies the need for faith. In the mirror of our own self-importance, we fail to see the image of God in which we were created. How blessed we are when circumstances crush our haughty spirits and give us a realistic picture of ourselves and our world.

Although God does not cause our moments of depression, He is prepared to use them for our growth. With whatever it takes to get our attention, God is ready to lead us on a journey of grace. Our most profound thoughts and invigorating insights are not the product of frivolity. In serious and solemn reaction to life's burdens, we seek the mind of Christ. We are conditioned to think God's thoughts only when we recognize our desperate need for a divine perspective. In humble recognition of our own inadequacies, we place our hand in the nail-scarred hand of Jesus. From His submission to the Father, we learn the significance of our own surrender. In His pain, we see the redemptive value of our own suffering. In many ways, we see a cross running through the complexity of life. Sooner or later, we all face denial, betrayal and crucifixion of one kind or another. Life has a variety of ways of imposing its penalties upon us.

Our greatest response is to accept adversity as an opportunity to be creative and flexible. God has equipped us with a capacity to deal with life's obstacles. Of course, there will be times when despondency and despair are inevitable. These moments need not be devastating, however, if we see them as a part of God's humbling process where submission and trust begin. Our somber meditation may be a time of greater learning, which leads to greater joy.

His Presence, Our Peace

The Bible begins with the words, "In the beginning God..." This phrase launches our most authentic affirmation for the existence of God. It sets the stage for everything else in Holy Scripture. It is noteworthy, however, that scripture does not explain the existence of God, nor does it resolve the vast mysteries of His eternal operations. We continue to be awed by the dynamics of God's creation. We are often overwhelmed by the vast amount of goodness as well as the escalating evil, which converges upon us at various times.

We search the Bible for simplistic solutions and find that its heroes were also struggling to put life's puzzle together. Our Lord Jesus, while on this earth, did not say He had come to explain the world, but that He had overcome the world. There is a tremendous difference. In His humanity, our Lord himself was often baffled by life's perplexities, but never to the point of disobeying the Father's will. Amid the excruciating pain of Calvary, His words rang into the darkness, "My God, My God, why hast Thou forsaken me?" This is not to imply that God leaves us hopeless in the face of life's mystery. It means that while the perplexities of life are beyond our human explanation, we are never beyond the care of our loving God.

Perhaps in our struggle to adjust to life's unexplainable events, we grow more dependent on God. Our faith teaches us to rely on His tender providence. If we should ever fully grasp the majestic mystery of divine operations, we would lose much of our need for God. The proud human mind has a terrible tendency toward rebellion. Could it be a part of God's grace to use mystery as a means of keeping us close to the source of our salvation?

Let us not despair, therefore, when life appears to have more puzzle than explanation. Let us learn to love and lean on one another as together we seek the light of our heavenly Father. His truth is ever ready to invade our inquiring minds. His spirit will refresh our weary souls. And remember, His presence will always precede our peace.

Is this all There Is?

Sometimes in the scheme of things we find ourselves asking, "Is this all there is?" As life progresses we wonder if we have seen it all, done it all, and been everywhere we need to go. In a society, which exaggerates excitement, we often are made to feel we are missing something. The world of merchandising is always wanting to sell us something. It preys on our irresistible urge for more and better things out of life. There is a sense in which our economy thrives on our restless pursuits.

While there is nothing wrong with having things and doing things, there must be a larger definition of life. Jesus said that life does not consist only in the abundance of things possessed. There is a spiritual aspect to our being which must not be neglected. The tangible gains its meaning from the intangible. The natural derives its beauty from the supernatural. The material has no value apart from the spiritual. There must be more to us than surface appearances. Physical beauty is only skin deep. Affluence is only a facade. Intelligence is not necessarily wisdom. What is seen is not always who we are.

The bottom line is where the human soul and God intersect. We are created with a need for divine companionship. We hunger for righteousness and we detest our unrighteous inclinations. Love is the goal of our lives even though hate complicates our affections. Faith is the victory while doubt contributes to many of our failures. We struggle for peace amid the discomfort of despair. Heaven is our home, but we cling tenaciously to this earthly domain. We are not sure of the unknown, and for this reason we try to create our own castles of comfort and convenience. The search for God is in everything we do. Our need to be noticed, our need to succeed, our need to find pleasure, and our need to be needed are all expressions of our search for something beyond ourselves.

Where, then, do we find relief for this quest of our souls? Are there answers to the question "Is this all there is?" The Bible reminds us that if we search for God we shall find Him when we have searched for Him with all our heart. God is present in our daily fulfillment. He gives us contentment for jobs well done. He is satisfied with us when grace is received and given. The quest never ends, but we can grow in God's grace and glory.

Love's Power

How does love prove its power so that hate does not appear to have the advantage? How does that which is self-giving get the attention it deserves? How does unassuming humility take precedence over pride's publicity? How does the good news of grace become as attractive as the bad news of disgrace? While these are questions, which appeal to our human curiosity, they do not reflect our deepest understanding of these topics.

Love does not need to prove its power. It is power. It is the energy of sheer goodness. Love that is out to prove something will quickly turn to hate if its point is ignored. Self-giving does not need attention. It loses itself in the cause for which sacrifices are made. It works behind the scenes so as not to distract from the issues, which are uppermost. Humility never seeks the headlines. It does not even advertise its lowliness lest the power of pride invade a contrite heart.

Humility is a vulnerable virtue. No one can truly be humble without some reason to be proud, otherwise he or she is simply inferior. The good news of grace never uses the methods of the world to project its message. It is attractive only to those who have eyes to see and ears to hear. Grace receives its appeal by the power of the Holy Spirit and not the energy of manipulation.

The gospel is never in competition with the newsstand. Grace is always a superior word from God and does not need sensational headlines nor tricky advertisement. What then do we say? It is love, self-giving, humility and grace that will survive and those who lose their life in them will find the abundant life.

On Being Consistent

One of the most imposing challenges of the Christian life is the ability to be consistent. In many ways, we are all walking paradoxes. There are often strange contradictions in our Christian behavior as well as our Christian conversation. We study God's word and we try to hide His laws in our hearts, yet somehow we are never able to fully perform in keeping with His will. Our spiritual ambition is to be Godly, but we often reflect that which is Satanic. We tend to live in the tension of what we know is right and the reality of what we actually do. Our conduct is characterized more by our selfish inclinations than by the sacrificial love of Jesus. We want to be servants, but we act like masters. We love the Lord, yet we despise some of His people. We search the scriptures for eternal life and then use them as a vehicle for debate. We want God to be patient with us in our iniquity, yet we harshly judge others who equally qualify for His grace.

The truth of the matter is we are inconsistent creatures struggling to be stable and compatible with God's will for our lives. Even though, at times, our Christian talk and our Christian walk are not the same, there is hope. The fact that we struggle to be consistent is evidence of the Holy Spirit's activity. There is hope in the sincerity of our repentance as we share our frustrations with God.

Our Lord Jesus understands what it is like to be human and thus He longs to lead us "in the paths of righteousness for His name's sake." Our Lord does not condone our fickle faith, but He does encourage us to believe that we can be more than what we have been. Sometimes we feel like crying with the apostle Paul, "Who shall deliver me from the body of this death?" His answer and our answer is, "through Jesus Christ our Lord." To confess our inconsistencies is to discover divine resources and forgiveness.

Poverty

Poverty has a devastating effect upon the human personality. It robs a person of the ability to provide life's essentials. It takes away the dignity of paying one's way. It forces a sense of dependency with an embarrassing need to beg. It incarcerates a person within the confines of a very limited lifestyle. The pain of poverty is an endless cycle of frustration. Its victims are forced to travel on a one-way street to nowhere. The daily debt increases beyond any hope of repayment.

Poverty is a terrible state of existence and few, if any, who read these lines, will ever know the depth of its devastation. We are a privileged people indeed to be able to pay for that which we desire. We are doubly blessed when there is discipline expressed toward the things we want. We receive a triple blessing when, out of the context of our own affluency; we share generously with those in need.

There are some spiritual lessons for us to learn from those caught in the throes of financial poverty. They remind us not only of our need to share, but they remind us of our need to be humble. No Christian can gloat in his or her prosperity as long as there are those who live without the necessities of life. Humility toward that which we have will always produce sacrificial giving.

We also learn from those in need a lesson about our soul's deficiency. The shattering devastation of financial poverty is but a parable of the kind of spiritual destitution we have before God. We are nothing and we have nothing without Him. Only in Christ Jesus can we know the wealth of His love and the riches of His grace. Only as we humbly place our prosperity in the context of God's holy will can we know what Jesus meant when He said, "Blessed are the poor in spirit, for theirs is the kingdom of God." With pure motivations we trust in God to give us the desires of our hearts.

The Bible

It is important for Christian folk, who place so much validity on the Bible, to understand why it is such a vital book. In fact, our deeper appreciation of the scriptures rises in relation to our understanding of the kind of book it is. Once we grasp the enormous magnitude of this God-breathed revelation we can never minimize its word for our lives. We call it the Word of God for indeed it clarifies His nature and makes known His will. No other literature gives us a historical as well as a devotional perspective on the things of God. The Bible shows us the interaction of God in human affairs and we see it as salvation history. The music of its message draws us to God in a sense of worship and praise. The Bible is the tangible source to which we turn for divine instruction and inspiration.

Of course it does not give us answers to all the issues of life. It does give us, however, a mental attitude and a spiritual disposition with which to approach life's complexities. The Bible teaches us to be honest about our ignorance and humble about our knowledge. Because we do not know everything, we stand in the shadow of this great body of truth and allow its all-encompassing presence to dictate the direction of our thoughts and behavior. We study it, not for the purpose of angry argumentation but sincere edification. We lose its sense of grace when we approach the Bible as though we have the only interpretation. God is much bigger than any thoughts we may compose about Him. At best our Biblical interpretations are limited, and for this reason we must draw from the insights and opinions of others.

In the formation of our scriptural convictions, we need the Holy Spirit to give us a teachable and tolerant mentality. We must not try to own this Word of God lest it becomes an idol, which we control and manipulate. We finger lovingly the pages of holy writ, not for the purpose of worshiping it, but that we let its breathtaking inspiration carry us into the presence of God. When this occurs, the meanness in our methods of interpretation is lost in the love of God who has given us His word. People become more important than projects as we sing in one accord, "Holy Bible, book divine, precious treasure, thou art mine." The Bible becomes the word of God in our hearts as we celebrate its unifying power.

The Father's Will

The words were piercing and sobering as He said, "Not everyone who saith 'Lord, Lord' shall enter into the kingdom of heaven." The statement caused me to examine my commitment. Many times I had prayed "Lord, Lord" as I visited the sick, witnessed to the lost, taught my Bible class, comforted the bereaved and expressed my love in many ways. "O Lord, I want to be right with you. Are my efforts not enough? Am I not sincere?"

His response seemed to flow like a mighty river of questions. "Are you using my Name to make a name for yourself? Are you trying to impress people with your own goodness? Do you use my words to shower your own hostility on others? What are the goals of your goodness? What is the meaning of your works? Are you enamored by your own success in being "spiritual," casting out devils and setting people straight?

The questions stopped and after a pause He continued. "It's the Father's will which makes the difference. His will that none should perish...His will that you forgive and be forgiven...His will that the hungry be fed, the naked clothed and sick and imprisoned visited and the gospel go forth to the ends of the earth."

I cried, "O Lord, I want your will to be done in me as it is in heaven. I want to serve you with an attitude, which demonstrates your loving spirit toward everyone. I confess my inadequacies and my awkward feelings toward those who judge me unfairly. I want nothing more than to be all you are calling me to be and to serve the heavenly Father in the spirit of the Father."

I listened, for I needed a word of encouragement. Quietly it reverberated through my soul, "Well done thou good and faithful servant, enter into the joys of your Lord." A happy sensation overwhelmed me as my struggling soul confessed an authentic faith. Now I have found the joy in serving Jesus. It is the Father's Will.

Holy Bible, Book Divine

It is important for Christian folk, who place so much validity on the Bible, to understand why it is such a vital book. In fact, our deeper appreciation of the scriptures rises in relation to our understanding of the kind of book it is. Once we grasp the enormous magnitude of this God-breathed revelation we can never minimize its word for our lives.

We call it the Word of God for indeed it clarifies His nature and makes known His will. No other literature gives us a historical as well as a devotional perspective on the things of God. The Bible shows us the interaction of God in human affairs and we see it as salvation history. The music of its message draws us to God in a sense of worship and praise. The Bible is the tangible source to which we turn for divine instruction and inspiration.

Of course, it does not give us answers to all the issues of life. It does give us, however, a mental attitude and a spiritual disposition with which to approach life's complexities. The Bible teaches us to be honest about our ignorance and humble about our knowledge. Because we do not know everything, we stand in the shadow of this great body of truth and allow its all-encompassing presence to dictate the direction of our thoughts and behavior. We study it not for the purpose of angry argumentation but sincere edification. We lose its sense of grace when we approach the Bible as though we have the only interpretation. God is much bigger than any thoughts we may compose about Him.

At best, our Biblical interpretations are limited, and for this reason we must draw from the insights and opinions of others. In the formation of our scriptural convictions, we need the Holy Spirit to give us a teachable and tolerant mentality. We must not try to own this Word of God lest it becomes an idol, which we control and manipulate.

We finger lovingly the pages of holy writ, not for the purpose of worshiping it, but that we let its breathtaking inspiration carry us into the presence of God. When this occurs, the meanness in our methods of interpretation is lost in the love of God who has given us His word. People become more important than simplistic pronouncements as we sing in one accord, "Holy Bible, book divine, precious treasure, thou art mine." The Bible becomes the Word of God in our hearts and we celebrate its unifying power.

Biblical Integrity

One of our problems with honest Biblical interpretation is that we want our Bible to specifically address every issue. We want it to give simple, pat answers to all our complicated questions. When it does not, we twist and bend certain passages to give us our desired result. We manipulate the Word of God to suit our own interpretation. The truth is, the Bible does not explicitly supply us with easy solutions to all our problems. For this reason it is dishonest to make certain passages say things never intended. The Bible is God's inspired Word on many issues and it gives us direction and guidelines for all issues, but a specific conclusion on so many matters is ours to discover.

In no way does this minimize the authority of Holy Scripture. In reality it allows the Bible to point to something greater. If the Bible had told us everything, there would have been no need for the Holy Spirit. Jesus told the disciples before His departure that He had much more to tell them, but they were not ready to grasp it. He announced the coming of the Holy Spirit who would lead them into all truth. Here then is our clue for approaching today's complex issues. We must seek the guidance of the Holy Spirit. Our Lord has not left us without a Leader.

Of course a question arises. How do we know our understanding is Holy Spirit inspired? For one thing it will be consistent with the scriptures. It will reflect the spirit of Jesus as He dealt with the issues of His day. There will be no malice or jealousy in the way we discuss our opinions. We will be open to what others have to say on the matter. We will be firm in where we search for truth, but not dogmatic in our decisions. We will leave room for the Holy Spirit to correct our mistakes and redirect our thinking.

A closed mind on any issue cannot enjoy the fruit of the Spirit. We are not sufficient within ourselves to have all the answers. We do not own the scriptures and neither do we own the Holy Spirit. We must allow them the freedom to speak to us whenever and however they choose. There is a wonderful peace in permitting the Holy Spirit to control our

Being Fed by Feeding

I went to the well for the water of life, but no one gave me a drink. I went to the cupboard for the bread, which sustains, and no one gave me to eat. My soul was famished and in need of spiritual strength, but everyone was searching to fill his or her own empty cup. I watched while others went frantically from well to well and cupboard-to-cupboard to find nourishment to suit their taste, but no one offered me food or drink. I listened to the language of those who were sound in their belief and in their behavior, but still no one gave me to eat. I worshiped with those who seemed to be happy and emotionally full, but their water they did not share. My hunger grew worse and my thirst became unbearable. "Does no one care that I perish?" I asked.

My inner hunger and emptiness were about to overwhelm me when a frail little person asked for my help. I could hardly believe that someone would actually ask of me because all I had left were the crumbs of a fading faith. At first I wanted to say, "Go to them who have more to offer. They are the ones happy and full. My well is empty and my cupboard is bare. I have nothing, absolutely nothing to share. Surely you do not wish to eat and drink from my limited supply of spiritual resources!" But then I thought, "Perhaps I could divide my crumbs." After all, I knew what it was like to be neglected by those who seemed so full of the bread of life. I could share my few drops of the water of life especially since I understood that kind of thirst. So I gave what I had.

After sharing those morsels, which were leftovers of my spiritual drought, a miracle occurred. Both of us seemed to find the food we sought. It was as though a table had been prepared before us and our cups overflowed. I no longer felt people were avoiding me nor refusing me food. In sharing my crumbs, I found the bread of life I needed. In relieving another's thirst I found the fountain of living water. I no longer beg. I give away and have found the abundant life. The words of Jesus keep ringing in my ears, "I am the Bread of Life. He who comes to me will never go hungry. And he who believes in me will never be thirsty. He who loses his life for my sake will find it."

God's Power

The power of God is a fascinating phenomenon, which everyone recognizes, but no one can fully define. What is this divine energy, which gives strength and substance to the creative process even as it empowers those who believe? How do you describe that which generates life and stimulates growth? Of course, there are no words, which adequately define the activity of God. When we have said "God," we have said all there is to say about ultimate power.

This power of God, this mighty metaphor of divine creativity, however, does not always conform to our human definitions. We are often prone to think of power in terms of dominance and destruction, whereas God's power has the ability to submit and save. Divine energy is directed toward righteousness and not retaliation. Mercy and peace have a quiet power, which only God can initiate. The strength to turn the other cheek, walk the second mile, and die on Calvary without malice and ill will has its origin in God. The force of forgiveness, with all of its redemptive features, is a product of God's holy grace.

Herein lies the difference between the power of God and the power of evil. Both have the ability to destroy, but only God has the power to save. Evil can only return evil for evil, while God has the will and the power to do good in the face of evil. Surely ultimate power belongs to Him who has the strength to annihilate but chooses, rather, to love. His power is never at the mercy of His need to retaliate. He never has to get even because He is confident in His desire to love and to save whosoever cometh unto Him in faith.

Although our carnal minds cannot always grasp the significance of His grace, we must trust His power to bring all things to their proper conclusion. We must trust Him to save us to the utmost because that is His nature and the thrust of His power. Our eternal security is never at the mercy of our temporal environment. In faith we belong to a God of might and miracles. Our greatest spiritual ambition is that we may be recipients of divine energy. Of course, we are never really strong until

Cleverness

Has God given you the gift of cleverness? If so, do you use it to please Him or to please yourself? The gift of cleverness can be a useful tool when exercised with humility and love. It can give eloquence to our witness and keenness of thought to our theology. It can enhance our ability to articulate the gospel as it reasons away the hint of heresy. The gift of cleverness has a ready word for a doubting Thomas, a helpful hint to a boisterous know-it-all, and a kind rebuke to a self-righteous saint.

Godly cleverness requires the mind, the tongue and the heart to act together in love. If not, the gift of cleverness can become a means to hurt and to humiliate. When cleverness turns cruel it has the capacity to devastate those who are not equipped to verbally react to its harassment. Just as an automobile is a marvelous device, but is so dangerous in the hands of a bad driver, so is cleverness dangerous in the hands of a spiritually bad driver.

Surely everyone stands condemned who uses the gift of cleverness to alienate and discourage a child of God. It is possible to be so bright that we are actually stupid if what we say and how we say it turns people into hostile competitors. Perhaps Paul said it best, "Love is patient, love is kind, and love is never boastful, nor conceited, nor rude." Blend that thought with the Psalmist who wrote, "Set a watch, O Lord, before my mouth, keep the door of my lips."

Religious or Righteous

Do you think God has given us His holy inspired Word to be a vehicle for debate? Is He pleased when people fuss about who believes it the best or the most? Did He inspire the adjectives and code words, which have segregated people into competing camps of Biblical interpretation? Is God the author of scriptural confusion? No! No! Surely not.

Do you think God sent His virgin born Son into the world so that we might entertain ourselves with theories of how it happened? Is He really honored when that night of miracles becomes nothing more to us than another way to judge the validity of one's faith? No! No! Surely not.

Do you think our Lord performed miracles of healing, signs, and wonders simply to create a climate of controversy? Was resurrection from death designed only to inspire theological conflict? Is vicarious death something merely to quarrel about rather than accept? No! No! Surely not.

Did the Holy Spirit come to focus our attention on tongues, fire, and super emotionalism? Does He give us gifts so that we might win spiritual popularity contests? Does He enjoy the religious statistical games we play? No! No! Surely not.

Did He give us the book of Revelation so that we might argue eschatology? Are mystery and symbolism and "last things" the only gospel we have? Is the unfolding of the ages merely a puzzle to exercise human minds or does God have a loving purpose? Did He give us the church merely as a pit in which to hiss at one another? Does our Lord get pleasure in watching us feud about who is greatest in the kingdom? No! No! Surely not.

Well then, woe to us if we misuse God's resources. Woe to us if we become mere judges of people rather than compassionate lovers of needy humanity. Surely, surely we all know who it is who would divert our attention from the content to the container. How clever the devil is

Imagination

Imagination is a unique and powerful aspect of our human personality. It emerges from the core of our being where thoughts and actions are created. Imagination is the ability to form pictures in our minds of things, which may or may not be real. It is a tool of our thinking process, which is often a prelude to whatever conclusions or decisions we make. In one way or another we are products of our imaginations. The critical truth, however, is that our imaginations can be of service to Satan as well as a force for God.

As a tool for Satan our imaginations can produce any number of evil situations. It can be the origin of our temptations and sinful inclinations. Satan uses our imaginations to make us believe the worst about people. By imagining that some folk dislike us we develop all kinds of unfriendly attitudes based on nothing but false assumptions. Our evil-inspired imaginations can create all kinds of fears and foes. It can make enemies out of our friends. It can create a climate for gossip and bad will. It destroys the foundation for fellowship as it establishes a pessimistic approach to life, which drowns our happiness in a sea of complaint and self-pity. When Satan controls our imaginations we are made vulnerable to all his devious devices for evil. We become co-conspirators with the powers of darkness.

On the other hand, however, when our imaginations are controlled by God they become a product of our faith. God uses our imaginations to stimulate our spiritual creativity. Through imagination He inspires us to believe the best about people. He gives us a redemptive vision of what can be rather than a depressed spirit about what has been. As God controls our imaginations He keeps our thoughts focused on things that are true, honest, just, pure, lovely and of good report. The power of our minds in the hands of God can make an awesome contribution to His kind of world. The decision is ours, however, as to whom we allow into the secret chambers of our imaginations.

Perhaps the Psalmist said it best when he wrote: "Let the words of our mouths and the meditations of our hearts be acceptable in thy sight O' Lord our strength and our redeemer."

Vengeance

There is a devious aspect of our sinful nature, which prompts us to punish one another. We endlessly search for ways to penalize those with whom we disagree and toward whom we have awkward attitudes. The slightest difference of opinion can become the catalyst for harsh and critical comments. For some reason we want a pound of flesh from everyone who violates our code of behavior even though we are not personally involved. If God won't get them, we will. We seem to derive a sordid kind of satisfaction on being able to pronounce judgment on that which we disapprove.

The need to chastise, however, robs us of the opportunity to celebrate friendship. Our nervous compulsion to monitor people's private lives creates emotional and spiritual fatigue. As frail human beings, we become weary trying to find an appropriate punishment for those we dislike. It is terribly exhausting when we assume a role reserved only for God. We are not equipped to be judges because we are not wise enough to know all the facts. Our desire to embarrass and hurt those who have erred inhibits our objectivity. Our capacity for any kind of compassion is lost amid the need to conquer and prove our point. We are much too sinful ourselves to become punishers and stone-throwers.

The greatest relief of our lives is to accept the truth that, "Vengeance is mine; I will repay," saith the Lord. Our Lord never encouraged His followers to be God's "Gestapo", spying on one another in a nervous attempt to purge the kingdom of any dissenters. He taught that tares and wheat would grow together and eventually the great, all-knowing Harvester would make the separation.

Of course the sin of all sins is that of trying to be God. Our sinful pride causes us to impose our opinions and judgments on others as if we had the final word. Our task, however, is that of witness and not tormentor. In love, our Lord calls us to be kind and courteous in the way we express our convictions and our concerns. No one is going to be healed by a hateful witness nor will they be saved by our punishing

Truth or Consequences

Ignorance is a terrible blight upon the human disposition. It is a part of our sinful depravity, which escalates evil. Ignorance confuses us with misinformation and causes us to react irresponsibly. It discourages us from looking at all the facts because the discipline of learning is a demanding chore. It is much easier and simpler to cling to our own misconceptions than to pursue truth, which might change our lifestyles and opinions. Ignorance tends to reward itself with more ignorance. The old adage that "ignorance is bliss" seems to be the goal of careless investigation. The less we know the less we want to know.

We lose our hunger and thirst for righteousness with a lazy mentality. Ignorance will never allow us the initiative to think God's thoughts and to seek the mind of Christ. It arouses distrust of anyone who is not committed to ignorance. It causes us to feel intimidated by those who are learners and thinkers.

Ignorance creates enemies because it will not permit us to learn enough about others to love them. It is the basis of prejudice and so much personal misunderstanding. How often have we had awkward feelings toward someone simply because we did not know them? A failure to get all the facts about anyone or anything gives ignorance a powerful influence over our lives.

Surely the essence of rebirth is that the Holy Spirit stimulates our minds to pursue God's truth wherever it leads. If we close our minds and refuse any aspect of learning, then ignorance has won. When ignorance wins, then Satan wins and our sins are complicated and confusing.

How much emotional, spiritual and physical misery is the result of sheer ignorance? The wisdom writers of the Old Testament are accurate when they tell us that knowledge and understanding are more valuable than silver and gold. Let us, therefore, try to be "wise as serpents and harmless as doves." To know is to love and to love is to be like God.

Mysteries

The Bible begins with the words, "In the beginning God..." This phrase launches our most authentic affirmation for the existence of God. It sets the stage for everything else in Holy Scripture. It is noteworthy, however, that scripture does not explain the existence of God, nor does it resolve the vast mysteries of His eternal operations. We continue to be awed by the dynamics of God's creation. We are often overwhelmed by the vast amount of goodness as well as the escalating evil, which converge upon us at various times. We search the Bible for simplistic solutions and find that its heroes were also struggling to put life's puzzle together.

Our Lord Jesus, while on this earth, did not say that He had come to explain the world, but that He had overcome the world. There is a tremendous difference. In His humanity, our Lord himself was often baffled by life's perplexities, but never to the point of disobeying the Father's will. Amid the excruciating pain of Calvary, His question rang into the darkness, "My God, My God, why hast Thou forsaken Me?" This is not to imply that God leaves us hopeless in the face of life's mystery. It means that our Lord Himself participated in our anxiety.

While the perplexities of life are often beyond our human explanation, we are never beyond the care of our loving God. Perhaps in our struggle to adjust to life's unexplainable events, we grow more dependent on God. Our faith teaches us to rely on His tender providence. If we should ever fully grasp the majestic mystery of divine operations, we would lose much of our need for God. The proud human mind has a terrible tendency toward rebellion.

Could it be a part of God's grace to use mystery as a means of keeping us close to the source of our salvation? Let us not despair, therefore, when life appears to have more puzzle than explanation. Let us learn to love and lean on one another as together we seek the light of our heavenly Father. Remember, His presence will always precede our peace.

Spiritual Recovery

The reality of sin and our susceptibility to its power often create the necessity for spiritual inventory. Time and again we find ourselves inundated by iniquity with an awesome hangover of guilt. Life has a way of wearing down our resistance and we succumb to those temptations, which appeal to our weaknesses. How often we are faced with a need to be forgiven and to have the cobwebs of careless living cleansed from our souls. The gospel reminds us that we do not have to stay the way we are. We can become more that what we have been. The discomfort of sin can become an avenue of grace through repentance and faith.

After all, spiritual recovery is what the Christian faith is all about. We come to Jesus not because we are so good, but because we want to be. If we were perfect specimens of righteous living we would have no need for the Christ of God to deliver us from all that hinders and oppresses us. If our love were more pure we would never need to struggle with hostile feelings. If our words were always kind and our deeds were always helpful we would never have to say, "I'm sorry." If our faith was even as a grain of mustard seed the mountains of adversity would seem like a peaceful valley.

Because God is not as real to us as we often pretend, we drift into periods of indifference and iniquity. Our sin separates us from the people and the resources, which remind us of God's healing grace. Therefore, the message of our faith is a reminder to ourselves and to all who have sinned and come short that spiritual recovery is not only possible, but is God's dream for all humankind.

The shepherd psalmist expressed it well when he wrote, "He restoreth my soul." Anyone who has ever walked and talked with God as the psalmist is aware of God's restoring power. It is the consciousness of God's will to save, which enables us to survive "the wiles of the devil." We are not mentally nor spiritually equipped to handle our sins all by ourselves. Unless we are open to God's restoration we are lost in our sins. Indeed, our hope is in Him who said, "Come unto me all ye who labor and are heavy laden and I will give you rest." "All who come to me I will in no wise cast out." Properly responding to these kind of promises will enable us to say with the psalmist, "He restoreth my soul." How then can we escape if we neglect so great a salvation?

The Will of God

The will of God is a phrase sometimes used with reckless abandon. We carelessly pronounce God's will on activities and opinions that are purely human. Just because we happened to have a certain thought on some issue does not necessarily mean God laid it on our hearts. Many hurtful and devious schemes have been advanced by labeling them "the will of God." We are prone to forget the devil has a will also and has cunning ways of making it appear sacred. Our human tendency toward selfishness and pride makes us vulnerable to the devil's deception. We must take care lest we erroneously make God the author of things the devil has inspired. In our struggle to know the mind of God we must make allowances for our own frailty of thought. We are never farther from His will than when we presume to have mastered it.

This is not to suggest, however, that God's will is an elusive matter, which He uses to tease us for His own enjoyment. He has made ample provisions for our search and rewards us with a sense of fulfillment when we follow it. The truth of the matter is, if it were not for God, we would never be inspired to concern ourselves about His will in the first place. The next step is a willingness to arrange our lives around what we sincerely perceive to be the will of God. Why should God reveal to us that which we have no intention of following? In other words, the will of God is vitally related to obedience.

Our hunger to know the wishes of a Holy God leads us to pray and search the scriptures for that which is obvious. We learn from the life and thought of Jesus what is the mind of God. We do not make the will of God a complicated mystery. We do not force awkward interpretations on things we do not understand. We respond simply, sincerely and in a Christ-like manner to the open-door opportunities life affords.

We will never, on this earth, fully know the mind of God. Yet, we can know enough to be followers and learners of Him who said, "Lo, I am with you always, even to the end of the age." As we relax in this promise, we cease to be nervous about knowing everything and trust Him who

Holy Bible

The Bible is God's fascinating revelation of Himself and of the human response to His divine leadership. Because of its divine-human composition, we have no other book like the Bible. It is imperative that we respect this word from God because it is our most tangible expression of God's specific will for our lives. It is not a word on every issue of modern life, but it gives us a powerful context in which to evaluate every circumstance life thrusts upon us. To study the Bible and to see it in its proper setting is one of life's greatest blessings. To understand the kind of book it is gives us a deeper appreciation of God, who inspired it.

In our haste to pay our respects to this word of God, we must not make it say more, nor less, than it says. If our pledge of allegiance to the Bible is only one of defense, we may develop a hateful spirit contrary to its teaching. The Bible does not need a nervous protectivism nearly as much as it needs a commitment to its content. It is possible, in our zeal to give the Bible the prominence it deserves, to develop an unattractive and argumentative disposition. Our best testimony to scripture is seen more in our struggle to obey than in our tendency to debate.

What we have in Holy writing is literature that has stood the test of time. This body of truth judges us; we do not judge it. Since the Bible does not derive its authority from us, we must be careful not to use it for our own schemes of thought. We must not pick and choose that which we prefer. Our recent arrival on the scene of human thought does not equip us to compose our own set of rules. Only as we are able to see things from the perspective of time can we make proper evaluation. The Bible gives us that perspective because it is inspired by God.

This inspiration gives the Bible a sense of continuity and the essential ingredients of salvation history. As Christians, the Bible is our book because it points to God who, in turn, points us to one another in a relationship of love and grace. May its flow flavor our lives with an intense desire to know "what thus saith the Lord." As this word becomes flesh through us, we can participate in God's redeeming dream for humankind.

"Agape" Love

New Testament love is the strongest force of the Christian life. It calls forth the best from us in terms of thought, feeling, and action. Jesus introduced the kind of love, which has no awkward agenda. It is not an affection, which seeks to manipulate others. Its only reward is an opportunity to love for the sake of loving. One does not qualify for this kind of love. It is a product of grace. Only God can inspire this kind of affection. Our human tendency is to love only those who have earned our attention. Our love is often limited to our kind and our benefactors.

Because our Lord's love stands in such contrast to our normal human devotion, a special Greek word is used to describe this Godly kind of compassion. The word is "agape" and it defines our most unselfish expressions of concern. We do not have a comparable word in English. When we grow in grace to the place of expressing some "agape" love, we expose ourselves to pain. When true love is demonstrated, it is not always understood by those with a lesser understanding of love.

Some folk will become angry when we offer compassion toward the undesirable. "Agape" love does not always do for others what they want. It seeks to do what is best. It does not lose its effectiveness by trying to please people but by the sometimes painful process of trying to help them. We often sacrifice the compliments and good standing with some folk in order to shower them with authentic "agape" love.

Such love is never crude and cruel, but it can be candid and courageous in its attempt to be redemptive. Speaking the truth in love as well as acting the truth in love does not always produce applause. It will produce, however, a Godly investment in the lives of those for whom we care enough to be honest and kind. Let us learn to love one another for love is of God.

Something for Nothing

In our day of high prices and modest incomes, our prevalent approach to buying anything is to get it as cheaply as possible. We want as much quality as we can get for as little as we can pay. Such high interest in current give-away schemes reveals our incurable desire to get something for nothing. In fact, the basic approach to advertising and salesmanship today is to convince the buying public that we are getting more for less. We are all searching for a bargain and those with the most convincing rhetoric gets our business.

While it may be prudent economically to stretch our buying power as much as possible, such thinking has little merit in spiritual matters. We cannot assume a "something for nothing" mentality where God is involved. He requires the total investment of ourselves into His kind of life or else we miss the dividends. Spiritual economics focuses upon such things as sacrifice, denying ourselves, cross bearing, servanthood and giving ourselves away. Jesus said, "If any man come after me, let him deny himself, take up his cross and follow me." In essence Jesus was saying, "I will give you the very best life possible, but it will cost you and cost you dearly." Jesus never hid His scars from a potential follower. He never minimized the cost of discipleship in order to attract a rich young ruler. He required just as much from His closest follower as He did from the obnoxious Pharisee.

Grace was never intended to be a free ride to glory. It is an undeserved love, which calls forth the best response we can make to such a self-giving God. Our response is insincere if we think we are manipulating God in order to get "something for nothing." If we love God at all, we do so with all our hearts, minds and souls. The Christian life is a tremendous bargain, not because it is so cheap, but because of what it costs. It pulls out of us everything that is decent and good where the greatest investment creates the greater return. God loves us too much to allow us to become spiritual cheapskates. We indeed cheat ourselves when we offer anything but our best. Without God, we may know the price of everything but the cost of nothing.

Suspicion

Suspicion is a terrible tool of satanic confusion. It robs us of our joy and confidence. It creates a negative mentality, which hinders our need to trust. Suspicion breeds fears and makes us nervous about life in general. It robs us of our confidence in family, church, government and all those systems, which sustain us. Although suspicion thrives on misinformation and half-truths, we tend to give it priority in our thinking. It is as if we have an uncontrollable urge to be suspicious of everything and everyone who gives us the slightest opportunity for doubt.

It is a terrible way to live and demands excessive amounts of our time and energy. Of course, Satan is pleased because as long as we live with a negative mentality, it diverts our attention away from anything positive and good. As long as we go through life always suspecting the worst from everyone and everything, we will contribute to the chaos around us. How sad are the folk who daily live with suspicion and fear. People who have lost their ability to trust are to be pitied indeed.

The damning sin of humanity is a lack of faith in ourselves, in others and in God. Our own insecurities and inferiority feelings cause us to distrust others. Our unwillingness to accept and rely on others inhibits our ability to trust God. Suspicious people live as though God made a horrible world full of horrible people who are out to get them. Of course, people will disappoint us, and circumstances will not always favor us.

This is where God's grace gives us an understanding mind and a forgiving spirit. This is where a Godly hope evolves that will not allow pessimism to prevail. When we know in Whom we have believed, there is no need for excessive anxiety because we know "He will keep that which we have committed unto Him against that day." Our suspicion and fear will be resolved amid the certainty of our own convictions.

Yes, Paul said it best. "Whatsoever things are true, honest, right, pure and lovely. Think on these things." People who always think on small

Simon and Thomas

The disciples of our Lord represent an interesting diversity of commitment and understanding. They came from a variety of backgrounds and dispositions, yet Jesus molded them into a fellowship of love. The unique contribution, which each one brought to his discipleship, teaches us that God can use a different array of personalities in performing His purpose.

On the one extreme, there was Simon Peter. He was boisterous, brave and bullheaded. Often he did not wait to think things through. He moved ahead on the strength of sheer emotion. He was not much on taking instructions. He wanted to serve the Lord but not always in the spirit of the Lord. He was quick to defend his Lord but just as quick to deny Him. Simon was a single-issue man. He loved his Lord, and nothing else really mattered to him.

At the other end of the spectrum, however, there was Thomas. He was a man who gave much thought to every issue. Because he would not always echo the sentiments of the group, he has been labeled a man of doubt. Thomas was not willing to say he believed when, in reality, he did not believe. He was too honest to merely flatter Jesus rather than make a significant commitment. He was committed to truth, even when it hurt or went against popular opinion. He was not going to fake a religious experience until he had one. There was too much at stake for him not to understand. If there were inconsistencies or problems, Thomas wanted answers, while Simon Peter moved full steam ahead.

The thing, which impresses us here, is that Jesus used both of these contrasting individuals in a magnificent way. He did not try to force any of His disciples into a disposition, which violated their basic personalities. Jesus gave a denying Simon Peter another chance with His words, "feed my sheep." He gave a questioning Thomas an opportunity to see His nail-scarred hands and His pierced side. Jesus exercised acceptance of a broad spectrum of people who were honest in their search for truth. Let us learn from our Lord, lest we hastily condemn those who come at truth from a different perspective.

A Strong Case for Heaven

Someone has said, "We are all going to die with half of our music still in us." How often have we seen someone struck down in the prime of life with many a song unsung, many a poem unwritten, many a chore undone and many achievements yet to make? Even if we live to old age, the melody of our lives is still playing with many chords untouched. The point here is; there is a sense of unfulfillment about life. There is a craving in most of us to be as productive as possible for as long as we live. Of course we will never completely fulfill all our ambitions. We will never reach our maximum potential in a hundred lifetimes. We are created with much more capacity than the proverbial fourscore years and ten can produce. Our dreams will always outlast our life.

For this reason there is a strong case for heaven. Surely heaven is a place where we go on living in the light of our highest earthly aspirations. Whatever God inspired us to think and to do on earth will have a heaven in which to find ultimate fulfillment. Our faith will not allow us to assume that our love, sacrifice, devotion and grace perishes in the grave.

Shakespeare's Brutus was wrong. Good is not all interred in our bones. The Bible's hope that "we shall know as we are known" and "we will serve Him there" gives an eternal dimension to the way we shall live.

Jesus said, "I go to prepare a place for you." We have every reason to believe it will be a "Jesus kind of place." It will reflect the quality of His love, the character of His commitment and the power of life itself. Whatever music is left in us will burst forth in a crescendo of praise to the almighty God and His saving Son. Whatever worthy dreams were left unrealized will have eternity in which to become reality.

No, it has not entered our minds what heaven is like. Yet, it seems reasonable to assume God has put a little heaven thinking in our minds so we can keep hoping, growing and moving in heaven's direction. Even our speculation on the subject can have some moments of God-breathed insight. Sometimes mortal thoughts must give rise to the

Wonderful Words of Life

Have you ever wondered what it would have been like to have actually heard Jesus speak? What kind of voice did He have? Did it have a strong tone of authority or was it mellowed with comfort and reassurance? Have you ever secretly articulated statements of Jesus in the way you think He might have said them? We are grateful indeed for the eyewitnesses who have preserved for us a collection of His words. To study these words of Jesus is to catch something of the spirit and thrust of His ministry. The kinds of words He used and the arrangement of them suggest that the mood of His speaking was always that of love.

Whether it was the cutting words of "Get thee behind me, Satan" or the quiet invitation of "Come unto me", the character of love was always present. From the Sermon on the Mount to the sayings on the cross Jesus used words to reveal the heart of God. With prophetic authority He used words to curse the barren fig tree and to chastise the Temple merchants. With healing power, He used words to castigate the demonic and restore health to the crippled and unclean. With instructive skill He used words to preach His sermons for the multitudes and give private lessons for individuals facing personal disaster.

With compassion and insight, He used words to probe the motives of all who came to Him and to offer them the truth, which would set them free. With prayerful anticipation He used words to communicate with the Heavenly Father and to bless those who struggled to find the Father's will.

With compelling urgency, He uses words to commission and empower us for world missions. His words of old motivated by compassion for the people of His day span the centuries to become words of love for us today. As we hear let us hide His words in our hearts that we may not sin against God. In so doing may the words of our mouths and the meditations of our hearts be acceptable in God's sight.

Getter or Giver

Have you ever considered what kind of world this would be if God were a "getter" instead of a "giver?" What if God had made getting the chief goal of His creation so that everyone created in His image would have His encouragement toward a selfish life? There would be no such thing as sacrifice because the idea of a Savior-God would not exist.

Forgiveness would be a relative matter depending on its ability to manipulate others. Love would only exist in the form of affection toward one's self. Faith would only express the confidence in one's ability to succeed through accumulation. There would be no such thing as sharing with the less fortunate and the thought of dying for another would be repulsive to say the least. The concepts of church and ministry and caring for the hurts of humanity would be ideas foreign to the thoughts of a self-centered god.

How horrible we say, if God had been oriented around getting instead of giving. How thankful we are that His word is a loving testimony of His sacrificial commitment to all humankind. With gratitude and praise we celebrate His divine compassion. We experience hope and peace, as we trust His eternal kindness.

We are so impressed by His unselfish love that it becomes the theme for our songs and the inspiration for our sermons. We join Paul in giving thanks for His unspeakable Gift and all the gifts that are products of His selfless nature.

Although we are grateful for a "giver" God we must take care not to let getting become the goal of our lives. Let us be done with our "getter" gods lest we lose the precious commodity of grace.

The Word of God

The word of God converges upon us in many ways to remind us of our creatureliness in relation to the Creator. At best we are limited in our understanding of who we are and how we fit into the scheme of things. We are not equipped to be God, but we are equipped to know the mind of God. Although there is mystery surrounding the Divine presence, He does not wish to remain a secret. We are invited to grasp as much of God as we are willing to seek. We are not left without resources in our search for ultimate reality.

We do not have to concoct fictitious characters and suspicious myths about the past. We do not have to worship the bizarre in the present nor do we have to fatalize the future. We have the Bible as the written word, which bears witness to Christ the Living Word. We have the Holy Spirit, which enhances our appreciation of both. Whatever lack of knowledge we have concerning the things of God is not because we lack the resources and one of those resources is the Bible.

Too often it seems we substitute the possession of a Bible for a relationship with the Bible. The Bible is more than a book. It is a God-breathed revelation, which requires a personal commitment to its contents. Reading the scriptures with the aid of the Holy Spirit puts us on a first-name basis with many Biblical friends. We put ourselves in their places and soon it seems God is giving directions to our own lives.

The Bible can be more than a theological textbook used only as a vehicle for debate. It can be and it must be a devotional guide to God. Here is where we get acquainted with God and He has access to us. Here is where the Holy Spirit confronts us with our inconsistencies and empowers us for spiritual progress. Without this intimate encounter with inspired truth our relationship with God is limited.

Although there are many translations, paraphrases and versions of the bible, the word from God is clear and unmistakable. We cannot plead ignorance once we have been exposed to its treasures. To learn it is to love it. To live it is to lead a life of obedience and hope. How well the Psalmist spoke to us when he wrote, "Thy word have I hid in my heart that I may not sin against God."

Mumblings of a Christian Jew

"Go ye therefore into all the world," He said. Does He really mean that? Is this a command or a request? There is a difference, you know. It is a big, cruel world out there. Rome does not deal kindly with new movements. Surely Judaism will not tolerate competition for her converts. Our half-pagan world does not understand a religion of love, grace, and purity. Is it possible for this good news to be absorbed by crude and cruel minds?

"All the world" would mean telling Gentile folk about Jesus. I think we should keep His gospel for our Jewish people. After all, we are the chosen ones. He was birthed and nurtured by our kind. It was our scriptures that predicted His coming. It was our prophets who anticipated a Messiah. Why should we share this good news with anyone but our own? There are a lot of Gentile pigs out there who would trample the pearls of His marvelous story. Did not our fathers teach us that such people were unclean?

"All the world" could mean going to dangerous areas of foreign countries. It would be risky going to places where human life is cheap. Barbarians do not understand "turning the other cheek" and dying on a cross, crying "Father, forgive them." People could get killed trying to convince such pagans that God intended us to live with love instead of hate. The remote areas of our world are not advanced enough to grasp this gospel. The only savior they know is whoever can help them get what they want. Loving one's adversary and treating the enemy with kindness are not principles by which they wish to live.

"All the world" means going to those close to me who have thought my actions strange since Jesus came into my life. It means loving my neighbor as myself. What I know and have experienced with Jesus can be shared with my nearest critic and my best friend.

Perhaps this is harder than going to the barbarians because these are people who know me, warts and all. I'm not sure I am good enough nor

Samaritan family next door. How could I ever step foot into their house with the gospel when I did not even take food when their child died?

Surely He did not mean "all the world." My, my that would include Gentile pigs, barbarian tribes-people, Samaritan half-breeds and the neighborhood riffraff. He must have meant it, however, because He whispered strongly into my ear, "Lo, I am with you always, even to the end of the age." I know Him well enough to know He would not send me somewhere without His companionship. I must confess. It is into "all the world." I have been challenged to go. Will you go with me?

Martha and Mary

The dishes were rattling noisily in the kitchen. Martha was getting frustrated. At first she only talked to herself. It was a joy to cook for Jesus. He was complimentary of her meals. Although He did not say much His frequent visits indicated something was to His liking. Maybe she was a little too sensitive in thinking Mary was not doing her part of the work. "She will surely come to the kitchen shortly to do her usual chores," Martha thought. But she did not come. More mealtime preparation noise did not seem to produce the desired effects. Finally, Martha blurted out, "Lord do you not care that my sister has left me to do the work by myself? Please tell her to help me."

The Lord fixed His eyes on Martha. He studied her mood to determine the depth of her anger. He looked at Mary, who seemed a bit embarrassed by Martha's outburst. He did not want to sound unappreciative, but the situation was obviously a teaching opportunity. He wanted to calm her frustration by giving her a lesson on priorities.

There must have been a bit of pain in His voice as He said, "Martha, Martha, you are worried about many things. Your kitchen duties have possessed you. Your meal is more important to you than my fellowship. You have chosen to feed me. Mary has chosen to let me feed her. She has made the better choice because physical food is for the moment while spiritual food is forever."

Like Martha, we sometimes get preoccupied with important things, but in the process neglect the most important thing. There is nothing more essential to our earthly existence than a healthy hunger for God. To crave conversation with the Master is the key to unlock our spiritual personality. Unless we have fellowship with Him we may never survive the busyness of life. The Christian life is a matter of priorities. The "less than best" is always sacrificed for the best. Somewhere along life's journey we want to hear Him say that we have chosen the good thing that cannot be taken away from us. It is a matter of living close enough to Him to say, "Speak, Lord, for your servant is listening."

Spirit-Led Conclusions

One of our problems with honest Biblical interpretation is that we want our Bible to specifically address every issue. We want it to give simple, pat answers to all our complicated questions. When it does not, we twist and bend certain passages to give us our desired result. We tend to manipulate the Word of God to suit our own interpretation. We will not accept the Bible's limitations.

The truth is, the Bible does not explicitly supply us with easy solutions to all our problems. It is not so much an answer book as it is a study guide. For this reason, it is dishonest to make certain passages say things never intended. The Bible is God's inspired Word on many issues and it gives us direction and guidelines for all issues, but a specific conclusion on so many matters is ours to discover.

In no way does this minimize the authority of Holy Scripture. In reality it allows the Bible to point to something greater. If the Bible had told us everything, there would have been no need for the Holy Spirit. Jesus told the disciples before His departure that He had much more to tell them, but they were not ready to grasp it. He announced the coming of the Holy Spirit who would lead them into all truth. Here, then, is our clue for approaching today's complex issues. Our Lord has not left us without a Leader. We must seek the guidance of the Holy Spirit.

Of course, a question arises. How do we know our understanding is of the Spirit? For one thing, it will be consistent with the scriptures. It will reflect the spirit of Jesus as He dealt with the issues of His day. There will be no malice or jealousy in the way we discuss our opinion. We will be open to what others have to say on the matter. We will be firm in where we search for truth, but not dogmatic in our decisions. We will leave room for the Holy Spirit to correct our mistakes and redirect our thoughts.

A closed mind on any issue cannot enjoy the fruit of the Spirit. We are not sufficient within ourselves to have all the answers. We do not own the scriptures and neither do we own the Holy Spirit. We must allow them the freedom to speak to us whenever and however they choose.

There is a wonderful peace in permitting the Holy Spirit to control our lives, even our interpretation of scripture. Love is a marvelous tool for learning. It equips our mind and emotions to discern truth and error without agitation.

Jacob's Well

It did not matter that she was a Samaritan, or a half-breed, as most Jews would have called her. It did not matter that she was a woman of ill repute who came to draw water at a less conspicuous time. It did not matter to Jesus that conversation with the likes of her would raise the eyebrows of the respected citizens of that area. She had hoped to get her water and go home without seeing or talking with anyone. Her sin had caused her to hide in the shadows of life. Her lifestyle could not stand the scrutiny of the public eye. She was already the topic of town talk.

As Jesus sat on the rim of Jacob's well He saw hurt, guilt and shame written on her face. He initiated a conversation with a request "Woman, give me a drink of water." She was startled to hear a man who appeared to be a Jewish teacher even talk to her in a public place. Her response was briskly stated. "How is that you, being a Jew, would dare ask water of me, seeing I am a Samaritan?" The cultural climate of that day was much too prejudiced for that kind of interaction. The years had created barriers of dislike between the two classes of people. A Samaritan woman could well be suspicious of a Jewish male who would make such a request. His intentions could be inappropriate.

Jesus, knowing who He was, had nothing to prove or nothing to hide. "If only you knew who was asking you for a drink you would seek from Him a water which would quench your thirst forever" was Jesus response to her surprised comment. "Give me this water!" she insisted. "Then I won't have to come to this place of public gossip ever again."

At this point Jesus wanted to talk about husbands. She wanted to talk about the best place to worship. Jesus explained that a time was coming and had arrived when the place of worship would be less important that the spirit and truth of worship. This prophet soon turned Messianic in the woman's mind and she hurried into the village to announce her discovery. As a result of her uninhibited testimony, many believed.

Have you encountered a "Jacob's well" lately where the water of "good-news grace" has washed away your bitterness, guilt and shame? Has Messiah helped you overcome the negative ways in which some folk describe you? Have you tasted the water that quenches your thirst for God? Come let us drink together of the Water of life.

The Privilege of Prayer

Prayer is an awesome aspect of divine fellowship. In fact, it is the heart and soul of our relationship with God. Although we communicate with our heavenly Father through Bible study, meditation, songs and worship, it is prayer that defines and undergirds each of these. Perhaps the greatest privilege of our Christian pilgrimage is prayer. How blessed we are to be invited by God Himself to sup with Him and He with us. The availability of God to our sometimes awkward and inconsistent faith staggers the imagination. Prayer is our access to the heavenly Father through His Son Jesus Christ. Without it, God becomes a distant deity with no invited input into our daily circumstances.

Prayer is the most personal and private part of our interchange with God. For this reason, no one can ever keep us from praying. It cannot be legislated either in or out of our lives. We can offer our private prayers anywhere and anytime we wish. It is a matter of desire and need to talk to God. Our personal conversation with God need not interfere with anyone else's religious freedom. God deals with each of us as though we were the only one with whom He converses.

Jesus made quite a case for private prayer as He elevated the prayer closet over the street corner as a better place to pray. Of course Jesus did not eliminate public prayer as a part of our conversation with God. On several occasions He offered beautiful prayers that He apparently wanted others to hear. Jesus did know, however, that public prayer could get twisted and distorted because of improper motives. Praying done to impress others with either words or piety did not receive high marks from our Lord.

Prayer requests that are made primarily to spread malicious gossip do not serve a compassionate purpose. Matters that would embarrass and discredit are better left for the privacy of the prayer closet. Prayer chains are not designed to be hot lines to the latest rumors. They are sources of intercession for the latest needs which can be discreetly announced. Prayers that intimidate and subtly boast of our own goodness fit our

Prayer, when used for its intended purpose, is nothing short of a miracle. To think we can talk to God about anything, anywhere, and anytime is super...no, it is supernatural. This does not mean our petitions will always be granted as we desire, but we are heard, loved and given what God deems best. Prayer does not always change reality, but it changes us to adjust to reality. Therefore, pray lovingly without ceasing.

Community Perspectives

A Worship Thought

Public worship is an interesting phenomenon of our spiritual lives. It has about as many definitions as we have people in attendance. There are hundreds of needs within a given congregation. How can a handful of worship leaders meet everyone's expectations in a brief time of worship? They can't. The Holy Spirit has to translate and communicate. Truth has to be internalized. Music has to be appropriated into our emotional being. Prayers have to be composed by everyone. We invoke God's spirit upon us and unless we allow Him to have our undivided attention, worship becomes little more than a few moments of boring spectatorship. Worship is something in which God participates. In fact, it is not worship unless He does.

Should we always expect people to come to church with something as serious as God on their minds? Should it be made easier for the Holy Spirit to capture their attention? Should folk be lured by some kind of gimmick and then zap them with God? Is it too much to expect people to hunger and thirst for righteousness? Must we first serve an appetizer or perhaps a preview of coming attractions? Has God lost His appeal? Do we need the ways of the world to give Him secular creditability? What is worship to the person who does not consider himself or herself spiritual?

Worship is an event that gets something going between God and the worshiper. It introduces the living God in such a way that His unconditional love is obvious and His understanding of life's pain provides hope. Public worship does not happen in a vacuum. It occurs in the context of people. There is a sense of belonging and being identified with the people of God. We are conscious of others and others are conscious of us. Worship is as public as everyone singing together, but as private as one's personal pilgrimage. If God is sought He can design a blessing to meet everyone's particular need. What a call to worship when the Psalmist said, "I was glad when they said unto me, let us go into the house of the Lord!" May it always happen for us when we yield our minds to God's truth, our hearts to His love, and our lives

Called to Participate

In our desire to be faithful Christians we spend many hours in church. Sometimes we attend and it is mere ritual. We go through the motions of worship and Bible study with robotic precision. Because of its routine we never seem to grasp the reality of what is being offered. Our need to be entertained and excited robs us of deeper thoughts and personal edification. We lose our sense of being involved.

At times we approach church attendance in the same way we go to the movies. At the movies we plop down with a soft drink and a bag of popcorn expecting the screen to give us some soothing moments of entertainment. If it does not produce to our liking, we are disappointed.

Church is different because we are called into a fellowship of participation. For it to have meaning we must share in what is happening. If we are disappointed, it is partly our fault because we have been given a role in the drama of church life. Whatever is lacking may be our own contribution. The truth is, "the more we give the more we receive." Of course, others must share equally if we are to have a vital church experience.

There is nothing boring or routine about what God has done for us in Christ. If there is monotony in church, it is a human factor. It stems from either disinterest or false expectations. To lose ourselves in the goals and ambitions of God makes church the most exciting aspect of our lives, however poorly it may perform at times.

There are occasions when our need to blame God for life's difficulties causes us to be bitter toward church and church people. Our anger toward God is translated into cries of "boring sermons," "poorly taught Bible lessons," "It is not like it used to be," and "no one has reached out to me." All the above may be true, but first we must determine how much we have contributed to it.

We must not give up on God because we experience a drought of spiritual zest. It too will pass away, and if we are faithful there will come a time when salvation's joy will return. Songs will sound as if we wrote them. Sermons will be like letters mailed to our spiritual address. Bible study will be autographed by God with our name in bold print. Old things will have passed away and all things will become new. Monotony will give rise to spontaneity. Joy will replace depression and God will be alive in our lives. This does not mean the valley will never return; but when it does, we can anticipate another journey to the mountain.

The Gift of Work

Work is the inevitable satisfaction of everyone who has the energy and the will to make a constructive contribution to human welfare. Labor for the law-abiding citizen is a part of his or her patriotic dream for a better country. One's career is a way of fulfilling the need to be a participant and not a spectator of life. There is a sense in which our work focuses upon God and country as well as ourselves. We work for God because it gives Him pleasure to see us utilize all the creative possibilities He has placed within us. He dreams for us a kind of success in every endeavor that will enhance His productivity on earth. He chooses to have no hands but our hands to labor in His vineyard of good will and human achievement. It is God's will that every able body and mind work to its peak performance.

There is also a sense in which we work for our country. Our land cannot be strong without the productive input of every citizen. When leisure and pleasure become an obsession, the strength of our nation is severely compromised. We lose a part of our economic soul when the talents and energies of some lie dormant.

Furthermore, there is a big sense in which we work for ourselves. In no better way can we realize our deepest dreams than through the skills with which we have been endowed. By the sweat of our brows we know the sweet satisfaction of being involved in life. God has given us no greater function in life than to graciously participate in that which we call work. It is only through honest toil that even our rest can find its fullest meaning. Let us, therefore, celebrate the gift of work and the resulting opportunity to know the inner peace of genuine fatigue. God's work ethic always ends with "well done thou good and faithful servant."

Education versus Indoctrination

There is a subtle, yet sometimes devious, difference between education and indoctrination. In our haste to teach, we can easily confuse the two. Education is an attempt to discover all the facts. It pursues truth wherever it leads. At its best, education exposes people with a learning disposition to all bodies of thought. It does not dictate what one should think but creates a framework of facts from which to draw personal conclusions. Education is the free and unhindered opportunity to discover the truth that sets us free.

Of course, research lends itself to much trial and error, but the end result allows learning to occur. Learning is not an easy task. It requires discipline of thought and a deep commitment to the subject under investigation. Education occurs when the mind is open and receptive to the many ways in which we can be taught.

Likewise, indoctrination is committed to teaching but with a more focused intent. Its purpose is to sell and promote rather than discover. It teaches with a bias toward some particular pattern of thought. It does not allow its students the freedom to explore other possibilities. While indoctrinators are convinced of the truthfulness of that which they teach, they can sometimes stray from the truth in their zeal to advance their cause. For example, communism in its attempt to indoctrinate sought to rewrite history. In so doing, it violated the basic principles of education. Indoctrination tends to stifle the democratic process where truth and freedom can serve each other. It can happen in the classroom as well as in country.

Indoctrinators are sometimes fearful of education because they are unwilling to allow their opinions to be scrutinized by all the facts. Religion is terribly vulnerable to rigid indoctrinators who wish to coerce and manipulate people's minds. Even in theological thought there must be a way to turn the other cheek and to go the second mile. Education is never a completed process. As we are being educated

God's Diversity

There is an interesting diversity in my backyard. On any given morning a variety of creatures help themselves to whatever it has to offer. A rabbit nibbles on the tender grass near the garden. Two or three squirrels search for nuts they hid for a later meal. Birds such as robins, blue jays, cardinals, finches and an assortment of feathered friends work the trees and grass. Occasionally a chipmunk will seek sunlight and food before going underground again.

The fascinating thing about my mini-zoo is how well its inhabitants accept one another. The rabbit doesn't mind sharing the yard with squirrels and birds. The birds seem to have no problem that among them are red, blue, brown and black species. All the animals accept the diversity of that part of their world.

Would that we humans could make a similar adjustment to the beautiful variety that exists among us. There is surely such a place and a plan for each of us in God's economy. His will is that we share the backyards of our lives with whoever is there.

Occasionally the neighbor's cat strolls across my lawn. His presence sends squirrels scurrying up the trees, birds retreating to the highest limbs, rabbits running into the brush, and chipmunks burrowing into their holes. They all run because the cat is an animal of prey. He will not allow them the freedom to roam my yard. In fear they adjust their lifestyles when the cat is around.

Some people are predators also. They do not accept diversity. They want to eat and devour those who are different. They want the backyard to have only their kind of creatures. Some of these folk are religious predators who hate and harm in the name of their god. They send people hurrying to their hiding places in order to escape rigidity and judgmental dispositions.

My backyard is a parable. It reminds me that I live in God's backyard, and He wants me to accept and share His delight in the variety of folk who use it. Perhaps my backyard is teaching me what true religion is all about. I must reach out to all kinds of people and share the love God has graciously given.

Money

Money is a fickle "god" because it demands an awesome sacrifice in terms of time and energy to acquire it, but it never quite produces that for which we dream. The price tag for life's true economy is measured by more than dollars and cents. The investment portfolio for lasting security includes more than stocks and bonds. Although money is essential to the survival of life, it does not meet our deepest needs. There is no way to finance real happiness. A good conscience is not a commodity to be charged to our credit card. There is no market in which we can buy peace of mind. There is no insurance policy against the possibility of troubles and trials.

Whatever value money may have for us is derived from our commitment to the things which money cannot buy. It is a happy person indeed who sees money in the context of God's grace. None of us is worthy of God's material blessings, yet He has allowed most of us some measure of economic security. It is a reason for real humility when we fully grasp how fragile and dependent is our human existence. Were it not for such things as health, education, family and other opportunities over which we have little or no control, we could not survive.

Of course, we have to adjust and cooperate with life's circumstances, but the bottom line of it all is that God has been good to us. To understand and appreciate God's benevolent attention toward us is the beginning of Christian stewardship. A financial commitment to God is more than just a willingness to tithe. It is recognition of partnership with God, which affects everything we do and say. From this perspective, money is not in competition with God. It becomes His servant and a means for our continuing discipleship. Our spiritual as well as our physical survival may be indexed by the use of our money.

On Being Family

In the beginning when God created Adam and Eve as the original parents of the human race. He instilled the sense of family. As people began to populate the earth dependency was soon observed. Children needed parents to nurture and sustain them until they could nurture and sustain themselves. Parents needed children to care for them in their declining years. Larger families began to develop and patriarchs presided over and protected the several families of their offspring. The concept of tribe reached out and brought together all the families of a certain ancestor. Tribes came together to form nations of people with a common heritage. Civilization became a complex intermingling of families, tribes, and kin of all kinds. History emerged as a focus on the family where the continuity of ancestors was studied.

Thus we see from the beginning of time family has been vital to the survival of the human race. It is the basic unit of organized society. God intended for us to be family before we could ever be tribe or nation. The strength of all our combined families determines the strength of our nation. It is family that creates the setting for stability within our country. Wisdom, decency, and honesty are established in the family. Parents have the best chance to make a positive influence on the world by the way they rear their offspring. Moral and spiritual values are instilled early in life or they may never be instilled at all.

Of course, families can contribute to the deterioration of a nation. If the family is corrupt it will corrupt society. The lack of discipline at home by both parents and children has a demoralizing effect upon everyone whose life they intersect. Hostility developed at home in children often lingers for life and tends to complicate all relationships. The family has as much potential for bad as for good if God's purpose for it is not realized.

The God of the Bible is a family God. He reveals Himself as loving Father. He comes to us through His obedient Son. He mothers us with the tender attention of a mother hen looking after her chicks. He gives us brothers and sisters in the context of church and calls us the "family of God." He calls on parents to rear their children in the nurture and admonition of the Lord. He requires children to respect authority and to honor their honorable parents. The family atmosphere is one of joy as God allows "goodness and mercy to follow us all the days of our lives."

People Power

The power of people to affect us is an interesting phenomenon. We are influenced daily by what people say or do to us. Sometimes it is what they do not say or do not do to us that makes a big difference in our lives. We give other folk a big amount of control over the way we think and act. Our dispositions are often the result of our reactions to the way people have treated us. Our moods are made either better or worse depending on who has been messing with our minds. For some reason we seem to be programmed to let others determine if we are to be happy or sad.

We are incurably addicted to what others think about us. We give away our freedom to be our own person in hopes that we can be liked by other persons. It can be an awkward way to live if we are intimidated continually by the power of people and never find our real identity. The strong influence of other people however does not need to be a negative factor in our lives. We can be motivated and challenged to do our best because they expect it of us. We can get a better picture of who we are from those who love us enough to share their honest opinions.

A certain amount of praise and congratulations are essential to our good self-image. We need others to encourage us on the journey of life. We must have the reinforcements of people lest we lose ourselves in a pool of self-pity. We need teachers, mentors, critics, spouses, family, and a supporting cast of folk to keep us on course.

We do not have to give away our identity, but we can give away our pride. Before significant others we can be humble without being humiliated. We can lean on others without losing our self-respect. The laughter of others can lift our spirits. Even the scorn of others can challenge our stamina. We can indeed be indebted to others without losing our will to win.

Since we are surrounded by a multiplicity of people, the Lord God of everyone wants us to find our place. We are not lost in the crowd. We are energized by His grace and inspired by His people. We look down

Picky People

When Jesus said, "Judge not that you be not judged," He was encouraging us to review the repercussions of being judgmental. Harsh and critical folk make themselves vulnerable to public scrutiny. The kind of evaluations we make of others is usually the kind of evaluation we receive. In other words, "what goes around comes around." If we are "picky, picky" people then, most likely, we are going to be picked at with a similar pickiness. Opinionated folk who are always making the latest pronouncements on everything are required to live up to their impressive knowledge.

Being judgmental implies a righteousness most of us do not have. Our inconsistencies become glaringly obvious when we try to advertise the discrepancies of others. No one is more eager to dig up our dirt than those whose dirt we have exposed. It seems to be a human tendency to return dirt for dirt.

Probably the most obnoxious people we know are those who are always trying to set other people straight. To be honest, we often feel a little satisfaction when the cracks in their armor are revealed. It is not a healthy way to live because our focus is on the behavior of others rather than on our own behavior. We get sidetracked into peripheral issues, which greatly hinder our opportunities to witness. Our most effective sharing of Christ is not done from a super-Christian mentality but from a humble disposition of shared grace. A superior attitude is a breeding ground for bitterness and resentment.

Jesus knew that the only way to stop the cycle of hate and verbal retaliations was to discourage a judgmental disposition. Christian love, fellowship and witness are greatly enhanced when we resign from the "god business." Personal relationships thrive when we are honest about who we are and kind about who others are. The truth of the matter is we never know enough to be judges. At best, our opinions are at the mercy of limited facts. Perhaps our most wholesome attitude toward the sins of others comes from the lips of our Lord. "Neither do I condemn you. Go and sin no more."

Defining Neighbor

It was a hard saying when Jesus insisted that we love our neighbor as ourselves. We are not sure we want to share ourselves that extensively with anyone. Jesus further complicated the matter with His broad definition of neighbor. In fact, He exempted no one from being neighbor if they had need of our attention and our resources. Our human desire is for a rule that would release us from our responsibility for certain folk. We want to know how far away a person should be before he or she is no longer considered a neighbor.

If geography is the criteria, then perhaps down the street and around the corner is far enough to be neighbor-free. If distance is defined in terms of belief, then perhaps those with different ideas, strange customs or no belief at all can be excluded from our required list of neighbors. Does only compatibility of thought qualify a person for our benevolence?

If race and politics and social circumstances can create a legitimate distance, then perhaps a lot of "un-desirables" can be treated as non-neighbors. If poverty is our plight, we may excuse ourselves from being neighbor to the more affluent. In whatever way we may wish to define and/or distance ourselves from our neighbor we cannot ignore our Lord's simple formula.

To Jesus, neighbor had nothing to do with geography, or creed, or race, or any set of circumstances. It was a matter of being at a place and at a time when our resources and our compassions were adequate to meet someone's need. No one has to qualify to be our neighbor. At its best, being a neighbor is a lot like grace. We reach into the depth of our being and find a reason to reach out to the best of our ability.

No one teaches us to be neighbor. It is a part of who we are in Christ Jesus. Our commitment to Him causes us to empathize with hurting humanity. His Holy Spirit causes our hearts to be broken by the things that break the heart of God. We grow to have a mind in us, which is the mind of Christ toward the needs of others.

we share life cultivate our opportunities to be neighbor. Some folk are our neighbors because they fit a certain criteria for closeness. In a more Biblical sense, however, others are our neighbors because of their great need of us in a given situation. The neighborhood is the world and yet our neighborliness is as focused as our next occasion to find a need and reach out in love to address it.

Communication

The art of communication is one of the great gifts of the Holy Spirit. Although the New Testament does not list communication as one of the specific gifts of the Holy Spirit, it does teach that where the Holy Spirit is operative there is love and unity. In other words, the Holy Spirit helps us understand one another. He keeps our lines of communication open by keeping us on the same frequency. In fact, He keeps us talking to one another until we have grasped the message each of us has to share. The Holy Spirit energizes our thoughts with love so that we are conditioned to hear with acceptance and grace. Listening with love is conducive to good communication. The Holy Spirit enhances our ability to say what we mean and to hear what others mean. The gift of communication begins with an appreciation of what another has to say. Being one in the Spirit gives us an advantage in understanding one another.

Misunderstanding, confusion, and hurt feelings are not the work of the Holy Spirit. They are the work of Satan, who seeks to engineer our misunder-standings. The Holy Spirit is not the author of confusion. He works in our lives to keep us loving and understanding even if the words we hear are awkwardly expressed. Sometimes there are meetings where it seems everyone is misunderstanding each other. The meeting is chaotic, unproductive, and everyone goes away sad.

 On the other hand, there are meetings where even difficult issues are discussed in freedom and love. The latter is the work of the Holy Spirit. It can be so in our interpersonal relationships as we give the Holy Spirit priority in everything we say.

Communication is not always a matter of perfect articulation or superior writing skills. If we are possessed by a cantankerous spirit we will misunderstand no matter how well the issues are stated. This is true in the proclamation of the gospel. It is not always the smooth, suave sermon that best communicates the truth of God. It is when the Spirit of God is present to make that truth come alive. The gift of communication affects every area of our lives. Let us pray that God will

Church Burnout

Burnout in the church and with the church is a live possibility for many folks today. It takes its toll on their spiritual happiness. They either drop out of church altogether or move to another church they think would be less stressful. Church has a way of overworking the gifts and skills of the over-willing. Some members have so much to do at church they never have a "Sabbath" experience. They get caught up in "church work" and lose sight of the "work of the church." "Church work" is hard and demanding. It requires leaders to be on top of every situation, to manage conflict and to deal with interpersonal problems. These individuals try to fulfill the wishes of a diverse body of believers and it is sometimes stressful.

On the other hand, the "work of the church" involves everyone in doing the mission of our Lord. The "work of the church" is a cooperative effort where love, understanding, and shared responsibilities produce an effective witness. The focus is on the many and not the few. We must all be careful that "church work" does not hinder our vision of the "work of the church" or else burnout will occur.

Church burnout may have theological implications. Some may do their "church work" as a kind of penance. It becomes an effort to atone or pay for their sins. If they work hard enough they hope to find some relief for their inner guilt. By doing so, they ignore sin's only atonement in Christ Jesus. Church burnout also comes to the overly pious. These folk overextend themselves in order to impress others with their commitment. Their struggle to be humble is frustrated by their proud intentions. They are so weary with "well-doing" they lose the joy of what they are doing. Unwilling to accept their limitations they lose themselves in needless guilt. Having no theology of failure they lose their theology of hope.

"Church work" sets us up for burnout because there is no finished product. It is never completed. We never reach all the lost. We never feed all the poor nor heal all the sick. We never fix people's lives to the point their problems are eliminated. We never learn all there is to learn from the Scriptures. We are unfinished participants in a task that is far bigger than our ability to perform. Because there is no closure to our task we can easily become overwhelmed and burned out.

The "work of the church", however, rescues us from trying to do it all, to doing all we can together. We do not have a finished job description because Jesus does not call us to a job, but to an adventure. Only God knows what it is all about. In His love He recalls us, changes our directions, and offers us new challenges. We surrender our burned-out souls to His rejuvenating care and do the best we can for Jesus' sake today.

Church-Worthy Trust

When church is really being church, it functions on the highest level of trust. There is no way a fellowship of love can be established without it. Trust is the ability to believe in, to lean on, and to accept the contribution of others as vital to our own spiritual wellbeing. Trust is the product of humility and inner honesty. In trust we confess our own inadequacies and seek to find in others as well as God the completion of ourselves.

In church we deny our tendency to be in charge as we submit to the authority of grace and a godly disposition. Church at its best does not have a dictator nor a clique nor leaders with selfish agendas. Because of trust, the leadership of the church becomes a servanthood. People are trusted to do their best and are given the freedom in Christ to develop their own spiritual personalities. No one has to become the religious clone of some super-Christian. Leaders are trusted also to do their best without imposing upon them an unreasonable expectation. Christian leaders are called of God to expedite His agenda. In doing so, trusting God and trusting others are essential for any achievement.

Of course, we make ourselves vulnerable when we trust. Human frailties and inconsistencies will often produce disappointments. In church, where we lean so heavily on one another, we can be hurt. A truth to be discovered, however, is that God will never let us down. If our trust is sufficiently grounded in Him, our trust in others will survive the pain of betrayal. After all, why does the Bible say so much about forgiveness and love and restoration if we are not expected to renew our trust in one another? Church cannot be church unless there is a willingness to trust those who at times even struggle with their own trustworthiness.

People Adjustments

Do you feel good about the people who are included on your list of acquaintances? Life has a way of exposing us to a variety of folk. Most of the time, we have little choice of those with whom we share life. We did not choose our parents and although we can choose a spouse, we cannot choose our natural-born children. We have only minor choices in classmates, working associates, and those with whom we share church.

Sometimes it becomes quite a challenge learning to adjust to folk in our lives who are there not entirely of our choosing. To some it may seem unfair to have been thrust into a pool of people whom we did not invite into our lives. The interesting thing is that we can add to, but we cannot take away from, this list of folk who have crossed our paths in some obvious way.

The other side of this thought is that we are on their lists also. They did not choose us any more than we chose them. Who knows, they may be rebelling against the process that brought us into their acquaintance. We must not assume everyone who knows us is going to like us any more than we like everyone we know.

As we reflect upon this fact of life, we see the value of our Lord's lesson on doing unto others, as we would have them do unto us. If we require kindness and courtesy from those with whom we share a bit of life, then we should express the same toward them. One of the greatest hindrances to good human relationships is that we expect more from others than we are willing to give. On the other hand, sometimes we give more than is required and become frustrated when others do not reciprocate.

It is a happy person indeed who can learn to accept and adjust to everyone on his or her list of acquaintances. No, we do not have to become "bosom buddies" with everyone we know, but we are required to treat one another with respect. It is a law of harmonious living to be

Comfort

Comfort is one of the great expressions of the Christian life. We are never closer to the disposition of God than when we seek to sooth the sadness of others. It is a painful world in which we live. Yet, we are never nearer to the compassion of God than when we have been crushed by cruel circumstances. God has equipped us to give as well as to receive comfort. In many ways the comfort, which we express toward others, is enhanced by the comfort, which we ourselves have received from God. God knows that we are vulnerable to the painful particulars of life. He understands the kind of grief, which often overwhelms us.

In our times of distress, God's most helpful resource in reaching us is people who have faced similar sorrow and survived. God uses others to teach us that "the valley of the shadow of death and difficulty" is passable. Through our own grief, God prepares us to respond with compassion toward others who weep. The extent to which we understand and appreciate the comfort, which we receive, is the extent to which we are able to comfort others. There is a stewardship of comfort, which blesses us as we give even as we receive. The trail of tears is a journey we all must travel at times. No one is immune to life's complicated procedures.

As we join the fellowship of suffering, our healthiest response is to learn how to lean on one another. By this means, the goodness of God is translated into goodness toward others. We are called to participate in the sharing of life's hardships where love is the basis of our survival. Therefore, we sorrow not as those who have no help nor hope. God has surrounded us with folk gifted in the art of giving comfort even as they receive the comfort we give. Our hearts are healed by giving as well as receiving God's comfort.

Despisory Vs Respectory

Once there was a man who found happiness and peace in the Lord. His new sense of contentment removed hostility and rage from his soul. He described his new disposition by the fact that he had tried to remove everyone from his "despisory." He used the word "despisory" to identify that part of him which had held resentment toward those he had chosen to dislike. The Lord Jesus had cleared his "despisory" so that he was free to love and respect a variety of folk whom he had formerly despised. How many people do you have in your "despisory?" What qualifies a person to be on your hate list?

Can you actually monitor the number of folk toward whom you have a despising mentality? It might help to analyze the contents of your "despisory" and let the Lord of love change it into a "respectory." Your "respectory" is that part of you with the ability to accept and appreciate others. The larger your "respectory" the less likely your "despisory" will be used. When your respect level is high, you have less tendency for resentment and hostility. You are blessed, indeed, when you are more inclined to pray than to despise, more prone to praise than to criticize, and more determined to like than to dislike.

Sometimes you may feel that you have valid reasons to despise certain folk, and there are certainly those who will be unkind and dishonest toward you. No one gets through life without occasionally being the object of disrespect and misunderstanding. You must never belittle yourself, however, with the emotion of hate and ill will. In the long run, you will be the loser when you allow your "despisory" to overwhelm your "respectory."

It was said of our Lord that He was despised and rejected, but He opened not His mouth. Surely, this is a reminder that God, Himself, will not cultivate a despising disposition even toward those who have malicious intent. For some reason, which defies human explanation, God finds a way to love even the unlovable. The Lord Jesus is your strongest ally when you seriously work to deplete your "despisory." It is

Dinner's Ready

Have you ever given much thought to the spiritual value of family meals? What a place for in-depth discussion on family matters and personal interests. It's not that the table becomes a place for confession, condemnation and parental sermons. In fact, if such should occur with exaggerated frequency, indigestion would most likely occur. Meals should not be mixed with trying to fix whatever is wrong with certain family members. Confrontation and argumentation can create a variety of heartburns. The family meal is a time to enjoy food with those we love. In the relaxed atmosphere of family togetherness, the act of eating has spiritual as well as nutritional value.

Whether God is mentioned at all, other than at the blessing, is not the issue. Theology and religion are not the only topics for wholesome family table talk. When there is respect and a healthy flow of conversation on any worthy subject, a meal can be as powerful as any form of public worship. Perhaps there is no other family activity that has as much potential for nourishing our bodies, minds and souls as does eating together. Daily bread that is planned for and prayed about makes the kitchen a sacred altar and the dining room a sanctuary.

If this sounds a bit too symbolic for our secular ears, then note the importance of eating in the Scriptures. In the Old Testament, every religious ceremony of any consequence was celebrated with some kind of feast. The gospels highlight the eating activities of Jesus, which culminated in the Last Supper. Coming together for common meals was a practice of the early church. We must conclude then that eating involves more than physical survival. It is a ritual, which has magnificent possibilities for fellowship and love.

Eating together can impact the family in a positive way. Yet, a recent survey reveals that according to those questioned over seventy-five per cent of American families eat less than ten meals together in a week. Thirty-seven per cent interviewed did not eat any evening meals together. Although there are some legitimate reasons for these statistics, nonetheless, the family is robbed of an important gathering time. It's like a church having a flurry of valuable activities but never pausing to worship together. Mealtime gives a family a reason "to gather" in the midst of so much which causes them "to scatter." A family who eats together in love will be doubly nourished for life's responsibilities.

Priests

One of the titles which the New Testament gives to every believer is that of priest. At first this seems a bit strange because we are prone to associate the title "priest" with the official clergy. Our definition of priest involves someone who represents God by serving His people in a special way. We do not think of priest as being a word to describe the total Christian population. According to the New Testament, however, as Christians we are all priests. We are called of God to minister to one another and to intercede for one another before God.

It is interesting to note that the early church did not use the title of priest for any of its official leaders, but rather made it an assignment to the whole church. Such priestly words as sacrifice, dedication, obedience and holy are words to describe all the people of God. Although the term is not one we use to address one another, we must not forget our priesthood. If we neglect or ignore our calling to be priests, then our church is seriously handicapped. We will lose our sense of caring for one another and being God's representatives in society. When we, as believers in Christ, truly accept our priesthood then our church becomes a living, vibrant organization. When we become priests to one another, our church is no longer defined in terms of the activities of a few "hired" professionals. It takes on the character of multiple ministries where everyone is involved. It becomes a free and creative fellowship where people are converted, comforted, and established in the truth of God.

If we have no priesthood, we have no church. We merely have a private religious club where we come periodically to encourage the "chaplains" so they can enlarge the club and enhance our pious prestige. We must not pervert our priesthood by being content to let others do our ministry for us. As priests not only do we participate in God's love, but in His delivery of love. We develop a caring community joined with other such communities to become a nation of priests.

In this environment of grace, we give as well as receive a priestly blessing each day. Remember that as priests it is our special calling from God to present ourselves as living sacrifices, holy and acceptable unto Him. We

War and Peace

One of the strange phenomena of human nature is that we are more easily motivated for fight than for peace. We talk about waging war, but seldom is peace as vocally declared. Our energies and our resources are more readily available for fighting than for projects of a peaceful nature. When battle lines are drawn we pull out all the stops as a strong appeal is made to pride and patriotism. Yet, our peace initiatives never produce the same kind of heroes as does war. "Bombs bursting in air..." are much more dramatic than a dove with an olive branch. Our evaluation of character is determined more by a fighting spirit than a humble appeal for peace. History has tended to celebrate its military personalities while crucifying the Prince of Peace. Of course we need to be supportive and grateful for those who protect us. We must truly honor those who have made the supreme sacrifice on our behalf. However, we must not lessen our struggle for peace in the process.

Sometimes our religious temperaments cause us to find a cause, which accents our fighting nature. We are endlessly looking for someone we can chastise in the "sweet name of Jesus." Why is this? Are our hostility levels so high that we are anxious to clobber someone when given the slightest provocation? Jesus dealt with this awkward need in the religious leaders of His day who were anxious to stone a woman taken in adultery. Because Jesus was more interested in purity through restoration than through elimination, He admonished those who were without sin to cast the first stone.

It is a master trick of the devil to convince us that our religious anger is always holy. There can be a significant difference between the hatred we express and the love we profess for the things of God. While Godly convictions must be strong, the spirit and attitude of Jesus must be stronger if His truth is ever to get a hearing in this world. It was never God's intention that the kingdom of heaven be advanced by the ways of the world.

He, who taught us to turn the other cheek, go the second mile and forgive seventy times seven, also told Simon Peter that he, who lives by the sword dies by the sword. Surely we are to conclude that a fighting mentality was not our Lord's design for His people. It is the way of the cross that leads home and love, not hate, is the way. Lest we lose our right to be church, our capacity for compassion must always take precedence over our terrible tendency to fight. Little children, let us love one another. OK?

A Missionary Moment

It must have been a stunning request when Jesus commissioned a handful of followers to go into all the world with His gospel of grace. What prospects did those spiritual upstarts have in making the slightest impression on that Roman world? The sheer statistics of such a command were overwhelming. The ratio of Christians to pagans seemed to be an insurmountable barrier to the progress of gospel proclamation. It was truly an awesome assignment thrust upon folk who only a few years before had been private citizens. They had little thought of leaving their own villages, much less going into all the world.

Yet, those rather ordinary personalities went forth in the name of Jesus to face the dangers and difficulties of far-away places. They were armed with nothing but the love of God and a compassion for people caught in the grip of religious superstition and fear. They did not try to intimidate nor argue with their pagan listeners. They shared the redeeming love story of Jesus and the Holy Spirit made their message believable. They were not fighting to keep alive the flickering flame of an old religion. They were caught up in the fires of God's movement and they burned with an enthusiasm, which allowed God to love the world through them. Those early Christians rearranged their lives, they sacrificed and they died that others might share in God's grace.

God used the loving ministry and witness of those first missionaries to call forth other missionaries. In fact, the whole thrust of the New Testament church is best described as a missionary enterprise. What an example those early followers set for us as their spiritual children. There is no way church can be church today without a sense of reaching out and going forth and sharing what we have in Jesus with others.

Of course, at times the task seems impossible. That is why we need God. We need God to help us understand that we are not peddling our own religious products. We are sharing His good news. He alone is the impetuous of the gospel enterprise.

Kindness

Kindness is often a simple matter, but has so many profound consequences. It reaches into the cracks and crevices of life's most difficult circumstances. We never know when our Christian influence will extend far beyond our expectation. Most times it happens when we are kind. In the common courtesies of life, we lay the groundwork for whatever witness we may offer for Christ. The influence, which Jesus has upon our lives, is expressed more by our kind and gentle ways than any other aspect of our faith. The love of God can never be promoted in a hateful way. All our loud and prolific pronouncements of Christianity are for naught if there is an absence of kindness.

Kindness is a product of who we are. It belongs to our personality. It rises from our Christian temperament and is essential to every area of our Christian lifestyle. Without kindness our commitment is nothing but an ambitious routine. Without kindness our talents are hidden in a maze of self-glory. Without kindness our testimony is lost in rudeness and ill manners. Kindness is the key to our most tender moments of prayer and worship. Church is a fellowship of love where kindness is evident.

The Bible is clear in its pronouncement to be kind to one another. A basic respect for others is at the heart of the Christian doctrine of man. Here then is our requirement to be kind, tenderhearted, forgiving one another as God in Christ has forgiven us. Therefore, let kindness prevail in our lives so that our influence will be healthy and our witness consistent with the kindness of our heavenly Father. May our ways be mannerly because our thoughts are Godly.

Enemies

How do we deal with our enemies? Now that is a tough one. Of course the normal reaction is that we dislike them. We discredit them and hurt them for hurting us. We tend to build ourselves up as we tear them down in hopes of conquering by our superior sense of importance. We divert attention from ourselves by questioning the spirituality and integrity of our enemies. Usually we prefer the more subtle methods of innuendoes and half-truths to keep our hate from being so obvious. We would rather camouflage our deeper hostilities in an effort to conceal the sinners that we are. None of this helps, however, because we know that it is not the Christian way to deal with our enemies. No matter how we try to disguise our hate, it has a way of rearing its ugly head to hurt us more than anyone else.

It is important, therefore, that we learn to appropriate the spirit of Christ in dealing with our enemies. Somehow forgiveness, love and grace must converge upon us to keep us from returning evil for evil. Somewhere we must gain the courage to stop the cycle of hate by receiving the last blow and initiating reconciliation. There is nothing more beautiful in all the world than eliminating our enemies by making them our friends. Of course the question arises, what about those who refuse to be our friends? Some people will reject us no matter how hard we seek a right spirit. Nonetheless an effort can be made.

The constructive thought here is that we can learn from our enemies and even grow in Christ as we absorb their hostility. Our enemies can keep us humble and dependent on Christ in a way our friends could never do. Opponents keep us alert to the fact that we are human and sinful and that our discrepancies are offensive to others. If it were not for those who dislike us we might never consider our personality weaknesses. Perhaps God can use our enemies more than our friends in our struggle with repentance and faith.

In the spirit of Christ our enemies will never really defeat us unless we give them that power. If our enemies refuse to treat us kindly, then let us make opposition our friend as we learn all God teaches through adversity. Our opponents can help keep us close to the cross where we will hear a familiar voice saying, "Father, forgive them for they know not what they do." Here is where we can truly pray for those who "despitefully use us, turn the other cheek and forgive seventy times seven" in the power of Christ. Let us make "friends with God's children" and as much as lies within us, live peacefully with all people.

Giving Others Power over Us

One of the phenomenal things about our relationships is the amount of power we give others to determine our own dispositions. We allow others to manipulate our reactions. It is amazing how we give other folk the power to make us angry. Often we surrender our ability to stay calm and collected to folk who do not deserve to have that kind of effect upon us. Often we are insecure and uncertain about who we are and that gives others the power to stir up our wrath. No one can really intimidate us unless we give them that power. When we feel put down and used, it is a matter of allowing another's opinion of us to control our own self-opinion. We have the capacity to determine how we feel about ourselves, and we must not give that away.

Hate is a terrible and destructive force. It often occurs because we ignore our potential for love. We give others the power to cultivate our hate by propaganda, mistreatment and dishonesty. We experience inner turmoil because we seldom consider the healing benefits of turning the other cheek. Forgiveness and grace are forgotten when someone triggers our need to retaliate. The truth of the matter is we do not have to give others the power to make us hate. Hostility and rage are within our ability to control if it is our deep desire.

Jealousy is another personal weakness, which we allow others to provoke. We permit those people who seem to have more and appear to flaunt their advantage to encourage our tendency to covet. We allow others to make us resentful about what we think we do not have in relation to what we think they have. Here again, we give others too much power to provoke needless jealousy.

Our capacity for contentment is within our power to control. Peer pressure is an awesome force no matter what our age. We give others entirely too much power over the way we think and react. The Lord Jesus is the only person who ever lived without allowing others to force Him into being less than his best. The Holy Spirit has come and dwells within every believer to help us have this mind in us, which was also in Christ Jesus. With his help we can regain the self-control God created us to have.

Hunger

The plight of hungry people in our world is an awesome challenge to those of us who have enough to share. As blessed and privileged people, we are under heavy obligation to divide our resources with those who have none. The Bible speaks a very clear word concerning the responsibility of those of us who have toward those of us who do not have. The fact that we eat and have some left over means that we are equipped to feed the starving masses. We cannot escape our Christian duty to feed a hungry world by assuming the government will do what it can. There has to be a public mentality for compassion, and we have to help cultivate it. We cannot relieve our consciences by simply denouncing those political and economic factors, which have created world hunger.

The urgent need is not judgment but mercy. Thousands of people will starve to death as we try to rationalize our unwillingness to help. We cannot hide behind a pseudo-spirituality, which says take, them the gospel and then they will be able to feed themselves. We must first feed them so that their undernourished minds may be able to hear and heed the gospel. What gospel do we have anyway if it does not concern itself with the whole person?

Can we hear our Lord on that great day when He says, "I was hungry and you did not feed me?" Our response would be, "When did we see you hungry and refuse you food?" He would say, "When you did not help feed the starving masses." Our reply might be, "But Lord, our government would not do more. After all, those people brought their hunger on themselves. We sent them Bibles and missionaries. Lord, we did not realize it was you. We just thought they were nameless folk amid the starving masses. We did not know it was you or we would have done much more." His eyes became sadden as He says, "Depart from me, you workers of iniquity."

Worship

Worship is a mighty force for getting something going between us and God. It has the ability to touch our most private thoughts and yet it calls forth our most public praise. Worship happens when, in the context of whatever we are doing, we discover God. Hopefully, it occurs in church, but it may be in the most remote areas of our lives that God intercepts our thoughts and inspires our dreams. In the quiet stillness of knowing that He is God, we may discover the turbulent winds of His Holy Spirit.

Worship is not always a soothing panacea for what ails us. It can be a painful confrontation with all our spiritual idiosyncrasies. If all we want out of worship is some moments of emotional "glory hallelujah" then we may miss the most challenging aspects of our encounter with God. There are both disturbing and thrilling implications to our meeting moments with God. We must be prepared for whatever His holy hand may write upon the walls of our hearts. He chastises those whom He loves and He gives indescribable blessings when we repent and seek His face.

Worship does not always follow predictable patterns. The wind of God blows where it will, and it is to our benefit that we stand in its path. Being in those places at such times when a God-consciousness is sought, we will most likely expose ourselves to the near side of God. In public worship, there is a difference between a congregation and an audience. When musicians, preachers and worship leaders sing, preach and lead worship with integrity for the glory of God, a congregation emerges. When such is done merely to please people, then all we have is a noisy audience of folk wishing to be entertained.

It is sacrilegious and vulgar; the way we sometimes package worship. We base it entirely on performance. If the show is good, we assume God is pleased. We do not know. It may be that God is able to use more effectively those who do not call attention to themselves even though their skills may have less public appeal. Some of the great worship events of history have taken place without a great deal of religious rhetoric and musical fanfare. Our goal is that in whatever setting we seek to worship, we do so with a strong desire to yield our minds to God's truth, our hearts to God's love and our lives to His great commission.

Reconciliation

How well do you handle reconciliation? Do you dread the process of making up? Do you enjoy clinging to the pain of past hurts? Does pride prohibit your assuming any responsibility for the conflict? Perhaps it is the discomfort of having to initiate the opening of old wounds and the cleansing of festered relationships that frightens you away from the peace table. Your hesitancy to apologize or suggest improved relationships may stem from your fear of being rejected. There are numerous reasons why reconciliation is avoided. Yet, it is one of life's most rewarding experiences. There is no joy like the joy of being friends again. There is no love like the love from someone who has been estranged. There is no peace like the peace of being accepted and restored.

How strange that something as beneficial to our emotional and physical health as reconciliation is postponed or ignored altogether. Sometimes we are our own worst enemies because we never allow our enemies to become our friends again. It is not so much that we keep returning evil for evil. It is the fact that we do nothing to aid the peace process. We suffer in silence and build up tons of unnecessary anger. When a relationship is strained we read into every conversation and action the worst possible interpretation. We sin against our own spiritual health by keeping a conflict alive in our imaginations when, in reality, a conflict no longer exists.

Jesus understood the dynamics of reconciliation and good relationships. In essence He said if someone hits us on one cheek do not hit back but turn the other cheek. In other words, someone has to take the last blow. Someone has to say, "Enough is enough. Let us stop hurting one another and begin to build a better relationship." The truth of the matter is that life is not always fair. Everything does not come out even. Sometimes we have to give more than it seems we get. However, when friendships are restored we all get more than we deserve. It is a grace rebate and a bonus for having the courage to go the second mile.

Guilt Trips

There is no good reason why we do it, but we all do it in subtle and devious ways. We put one another on guilt trips, trying to get each other to do and to be what we desire. Perhaps we all live with excessive guilt and seek to hammer others into submission with a similar pain. Our greatest ally in manipulating other people's lives is their weary conscience. When made to feel bad enough, most of us will do anything to buy a good feeling about ourselves. Our poor self-image makes us vulnerable to those who would use it to their advantage.

One of our greatest sources of unhappiness is our inability to distinguish between bad guilt and good guilt. Bad guilt keeps us forever in someone's debt. Our need to please keeps us in the throes of anyone who seeks to manipulate our minds and control our activity. Bad guilt produces emotional stress and serves only to disturb and destroy. Good guilt, on the other hand, has a redemptive nature. It encourages repentance and right relationships. Its pain has a healing dimension, as it becomes a deterrent to lingering hostility. It seems to be the nature of true Christian fellowship to use the energy of good guilt to create an awareness of God.

How sad when religion becomes a tool to badger folk into some kind of emotion. How doubly sad when the Bible is used as a club to coerce the spiritually naive. Surely, church was designed to be a place where guilt is dissolved by grace and a poor self-image is lost in an atmosphere of restoring love. Would it not be great if, in church, we heard only words of encouragement instead of pious phrases of a guilt-provoking nature? If only we could learn to help one another with our guilt, church would truly become a redemptive fellowship.

Friendships would be more lasting and family life would be more satisfying in the context of an atmosphere of forgiving grace. It seems like such a simple thing, but we disrupt relationships daily because we want to make people pay for their misdeeds and awkward words. For some strange reason, we want others to know that we know they are bad or wrong. What a different world it would be if we all were kind to one another, tenderhearted, forgiving one another as God in Christ Jesus has forgiven us.

Disfranchisement

The word "disfranchise" means to take away certain rights and privileges. It is to be cut off from some of life's events. Sometimes this can be a legal act, but most often it is a subtle penalty we impose on people who are different. There is a host of people living on the periphery of life simply because they do not conform to the majority norm. They look different, think different, dress different and perhaps smell different. For any number of reasons certain people are cut off and separated from the significant entity to which they want to belong. They are left out of a part of life in which they wish to be involved. It is a cruel way society has of treating folk who march to the beat of a different drummer.

It can happen in church when a certain creed becomes more important than people. When a pattern of thought and a theological position takes precedence over a kind disposition toward others, disfranchisement occurs. Church people who are so sure of their own righteousness can cut off those who they feel do not measure up. People who are considered spiritually inferior can feel disfranchised from those who enjoy flexing their religious muscles. There is a lot of rejection in church by people who ought to be the most accepting people in the world. It is sad when some folk do not feel free to participate in church because it seems to be for others. The tone of fellowship appears to be more exclusive than inclusive.

Home can be another source of disfranchisement. It occurs when material priorities become more important than family togetherness. Certain members get cut off in their search for emotional security. Their identity is lost in the struggle to maintain the family name and prestige. No one is more lonely than a family member who has everything and yet has no one. It is painful being kin to folk who do not cultivate kinship.

Young people are often victims of disfranchisement. Special little groups and cliques are formed to exclude so that insecure youth may have an the team develop deep emotional scars. Disfranchisement is a painful penalty for being different, especially if you are young.

God's word says, "Be ye kind one to another." Might we say it another way?

"Do not disfranchise one another by the way we talk or by the way we organize our friends." After all, life's franchise belongs to God and He says, "Whosoever will, let him come."

Friendship

How much does it cost to be your friend? How rigid are your requirements of those who would share fellowship with you? Do people get tired of trying to meet your demands for friendship and withdraw into mere casual acquaintanceship? Do you smother people with an overbearing expectancy that they conform to your way of thinking and doing things? These are the kinds of questions we need to ask ourselves when people tend to avoid us. Friendship is a precious commodity of human existence. Our need for friends is as essential as our craving for food. Our basic happiness in life is determined by our success in relating to others.

Friendship is a two-way street. If we want to have friends, we have to prove ourselves friendly. We cannot expect others to do all the giving while we feed our emotional and social egos at their expense. Of course, it works the other way also. Those people who tend to be parasitic in their relationship to us can never be counted on to stand by us when we need a friend. People who cling as well as climb are prone to use friendship to get where they are going. No one likes to be used or abused by either friend or foe. Friendship is a fragile phenomenon of the human pilgrimage. When we consider our individual built-in diversities, it's a wonder we could find ourselves compatible with anyone.

Friendship thrives in an atmosphere where there are minimum demands and a willingness to accept others for who they are. It grows as the result of a relaxed commitment toward a congenial spirit. No one is going to like what we do, what we say or who we are all the time. Friendship means we do not have to continually prove ourselves. We are not card-carrying member of anyone's fan club. We are free to be friendly with whomever because it does not bother those who are our friends forever. Jesus gave friendship an eternal boost when He told His disciples that He no longer called them servants but friends. How well do you do friendships?

Love and Freedom

Love is an emotion born and cultivated in the atmosphere of freedom. Love is a disposition, which does not respond to coercion, intimidation nor manipulation. Only when we are free to love will love truly be expressed. It cannot be sincere love when words are said and deeds are done out of fear or for the sake of appearance. Love represents the deepest feeling, thoughts and actions we have toward those people and things, which mean most to us.

If we are pressured or forced into a devotion we do not mean, then our lives take on the air of a hypocrite. True love is lost in the midst of an awkward need to please or be pleased. We learn this truth best from God who allows our love to grow in freedom. He calls, but He does not coerce. He makes His grace available, but He does not force us to receive Him. We are free to blaspheme or to believe, to persecute or to proclaim, to hate or to love. Of course, we bear the consequences of our choices. He allows us the liberty to fail even as He encourages our faith to succeed.

We must be careful in our witness, lest we try to be more successful than God. Not everyone who is intimidated into saying "Lord, Lord," will enter the kingdom of heaven. As we faithfully witness to His truth, the Holy Spirit will create conviction and the love of God will wait ever so patiently for a proper response.

No love, whether it be Christian love, marital love, family love, or brotherly love can grow when the agenda is one of dominance and pressure. Even God does not force us to love Him. Therefore, may we allow our love to grow in the atmosphere of a Godly freedom where we can love and let love be the spontaneous response of sincerity and faith. Remember, true love will always reach out to the unloving, the unlovely, and the unloved.

Commissioned

It was an awesome assignment Jesus gave to a handful of His followers. They were commissioned to share the good news of God wherever they went into all the world. What a task for folk who rarely traveled beyond the borders of Judea and Galilee. How could even God expect such provincial people to become world ambassadors in outlook and outreach? Those disciples, who had always narrowly defined religion in terms of their own race and geography, were now expected to expand their spiritual horizons. Not only were they numerically weak, they were culturally and politically ignorant of the world to which they were going.

How could they adjust to the diversity of thought, which had inflicted that Roman-controlled environment? After all, fishermen and their likes were not well versed in the religions of the world. They had no way of knowing they would be ridiculed and scorned by an unrelenting pagan mentality. It would seem that Christianity had little hope of penetrating the armor of Romanism with its sophisticated Caesar worship.

But there was more to those spiritual upstarts than a misdirected dream with a careless commitment to the future. Those men and women were for real. They had a story to tell, and it became good news to people struggling to find a God who really cared. The Holy Spirit was the impetus of their proclamation as they went forth baptizing in the name of the Father, the Son and the Holy Spirit. They taught the things the Lord had commanded them, and it made sense to people who had become discouraged with senseless philosophies.

Their hearts were warmed by a God of love who cared enough to send His only begotten Son. Rather than hopelessly searching the pagan myths for some divine revelation, they found hope in a God who would live and die for them. They felt the pull of amazing grace and it introduced them to salvation history.

The call still comes ringing over the restless waves to go into all the world and preach the gospel. There is no less need today than when that

Caring for Others

The most compelling task of our Christian commitment is that we do unto others, as we would have them do unto us. In no way can we escape the Biblical mandate to treat others with respect. We are not offered the option of retaliation, even when we are mistreated. We are admonished to turn the other cheek and go the second mile. In so doing, we leave the impression that love and not hate is the dominant force in our lives.

It's not easy being kind and considerate in a world, which equates meekness with weakness. It's not profitable to let ethics and morality control our aggressive ambitions. Of course, Jesus is our model example of self-giving love but who wants to be a martyr? We are not conditioned for the kinds of sacrifices, which our Lord demands.

We love our neighbor not as we love ourselves. We love our neighbor only in ways, which are convenient and non-demanding. We are prone to fulfill the obligation of our own needs before we make any serious commitment to others. The selfish satisfaction of conquering the competition inhibits our willingness to let anyone get ahead of us.

Somehow, the key that unlocks our desire to help others is discovered in the context of our needs. The kindness and love we require is the kindness and love we must give. Within the framework of our own personal needs is the best clue as to how we can reach out helpfully to others. We do not need a course in compassion nearly as much as we need to learn to treat others in the way we would like to be treated.

The best commentary on how we are doing is a sense of joy, which comes from our helpfulness. We are created for kindness and not contention. Our needs are best met as we proceed to meet the needs of others. To know ourselves is to know our neighbor. To know our neighbor is to express love in ways we wished to be loved. We are never nearer God than when we love those whom He loves. By giving us the power to bless others, God has equipped us to be neighborly.

A Prayer of Searching

God, I have come to church today
because I am desperate.
I am not desperate outside of me
where people can notice
but inside I am a dangling bundle of frustrations.

I am lonely and unhappy
and I am torn asunder
by the gnawing truth that I am a phony.

I have this terrible fear
that people will begin to see through me
and then turn against me.
Lord, I do not want to be rejected by them.

If I confess and repent of my sins
help them to be kind and understanding of me.
After all, I merely want to be what they think I am.

O God, help me to be authentic and courageous.
Help me to stop worrying about what others may think
so I may concentrate on being your kind of person.

Deliver my soul from the slavery of public opinion
so that I may be free and creative
in my commitment to you.

Lord, help me to deal with
my own insecurities and ego needs
in a way that would not embarrass your cause.

As I seek to understand myself,
help me to understand others.
Help me to learn to be patient with their sins
as I know you are patient with mine

A Prayer of Unity

It's a prayer of unity
that I lift to You this day, O Lord.

I pray for unity in our world
where conflicting nations have chosen war
as a means of settling their differences.

Give those who participate in such strife
a reasonable spirit so that hostile guns may once again be silent.

I pray for unity in our country as opposing politicians seek to
blame one another for our economic and social ailments.

Give those in authority a responsible disposition
toward the issues of our time.

May they turn their mental energies
toward solutions instead of accusations.

I pray for unity within our church,
as the lust for power is no respecter of institutions.

Give those who have a following
a sense of stewardship about their popularity.

May they humbly and responsibly
represent the cause of Christ.

Help us all to be cooperating Christians
in a body of believers who understand
that love will keep us strong.

I pray for a kind of unity where good people
have a right to disagree agreeably.

Help us to monitor our own feelings
in keeping with the spirit of Jesus.

Show us again and again that publicans, fishermen, zealots,
and a variety of folk can still function as disciples
of our Lord Jesus Christ. Amen.

Two or Three Gathered

In our world today of religious conglomerates, church has become big business. As we observe the electronic churches with their television personalities taking in their millions, we are tempted to ask, Is God for sale? Have we packaged religion in neat, syrupy sermons and wrapped it in emotionally draining songs to give it consumer appeal? Have we resorted to the gimmicks of Wall Street rather than the Golgotha inspired sacrifices of the New Testament? Have we allowed the search for mammon to hinder our search for souls?

Hopefully, these questions represent the extreme and the religious landscape is not what it appears. Surely the manufacturers of high-powered religious showmanship are sincere even though their product is sometimes shallow and misleading. Surely the people of God will become less gullible when they realize that para-church never becomes the full body of Christ.

It would certainly be unkind and unnecessary to discount any good from these hyper salespeople of religion. Yet, it would be devastating if that were all we had. We must never forsake the assembling of ourselves together as a body of believers to minister to one another in a humble, sincere and Godly way. There is something quite profound when two or three are gathered together in His name and God is present.

The Risk of Ministry

Sometimes we put ourselves at risk when we get involved in ministry. We make ourselves vulnerable when we witness. We put our reputations up for scrutiny every time we share the name of Jesus. Who do we think we are, trying to represent God? How can we invite someone to God's purity when our own lives are soiled? What message do we have to share if that message has not fully affected us? How can we preach if our practice is weak? These are questions, which often inhibit our witness.

Unable to accept our own imperfections, we surrender to a false sense of unworthiness. We lack the courage to risk our feeble reputations for the cause of Christ. Of course we are not worthy. Of course we do not know it all. Perhaps we have a false concept about witnessing. We do not witness in order to share ourselves. We witness in order to share Jesus and what He has done and is able to do for us as well as others. We live and serve the best we can, confess our sins, seek God's forgiveness, and invite others into the process.

Sometimes we make ourselves vulnerable to the people we seek to serve. There are folk who will prey on our generosity. Drowning people will drown other people, who are trying to save them. We must be alert to the subtle draining of our spiritual energies by those who need more than we can give. Loving another person is not doing what they want every time, but doing for them what we honestly think is best. The power of people to deplete us is a danger we must seek to avoid. Even Jesus turned aside for rest and renewed fellowship with the Father. Likewise, we keep our spiritual batteries charged so that our lights may shine effectively.

Another caution we must take in ministry is in developing a "holier-than-thou" attitude. It is easy to feel that our commitment is better and our involvement is superior to those whose works appear weak. In our eagerness to share Christ we can often sound overly pious. Our sanctimonious words may send a self-righteous message we do not intend.

The servant spirit must be evident in all we say and in what we do for others. We humbly respond to their acceptance or rejection of what we do in Jesus name. Sometimes we have to take the risk of being misunderstood in order to help others understand the love of Jesus. Sometimes it hurts to care, but in the long run it hurts more not to care.

Church

Church at its best is more than a spectator experience. It is a fellowship of people equipping themselves for ministry and witness. The call of God has always been for His people to be actively involved in making a redemptive difference in the world.

Church, therefore, is a learning resource, a training ground, and an experimental laboratory in the art of Christian living. Whatever transpires in the context of church is of great importance to every area of our lives. We cannot attend church in the same way we go to the theater. An entertainment mentality is not conducive to discipleship.

Church at its best requires a commitment to the higher things of life. There is no call like the call of God, which finds expression in the church. It challenges the moral and ethical fibers of our being. It pleads with us to minimize the things of the world as we maximize spiritual realities. Earthly ambitions are flavored with Godly motives. Love of self is defined only in the context of love for neighbor and love for God. Wealth is seen against a background of need. Stewardship becomes a matter of properly using that which we have. Ministry becomes the password of our lives as compassion grants us entrance into the hurting side of society. If we are serious about God we cannot leave events at church in the same way we leave the theater. A take-it-or-leave-it attitude does not produce commitment.

Church at its best is a fellowship of Jesus' followers. We do not go it alone. There is a body of believers to whom we relate. In the strength of togetherness we struggle with the issues of life. God calls us into spiritual cooperation where we honor Him by honoring one another.

There is a public dimension to our faith. Lest we become spiritual hermits, we sing some of our songs and pray some of our prayers with our brothers and sisters in Christ. Church gives us a place to observe and experience the operations of grace. The power of people energizes us to seek the will of God and in so doing we find a reason for which to live.

Church at its best is our most wholesome inspiration to do our best because "the church's one foundation is Jesus Christ her Lord."

Contagious

The word contagious often spreads fear among us as we think of some disease or illness that is easily transmitted from one person to another. We worry every year during the flu season fearing that we will "catch" the ailment from some coughing victim. We take multiple vaccines to immunize ourselves against any number of contagious ailments. We tend to associate the word "contagious" with that, which is bad about us. Mood swings, bad attitudes and personality flaws can create a negative disposition, which can be terribly contagious. We spread our emotional germs with critical conversation as we turn our backs on hurting humanity.

On the other hand, however, good things can be "catching" also. Perhaps we ought to focus more upon the fact that there are positive things about us that can be contagious. Is this not the whole idea of Christian fellowship? We come together to expose ourselves to the spiritual energy of the group. We "catch" our faith from one another.

Forgiveness and repentance are highly contagious in an atmosphere of grace. Love is easily transmitted to one another when it reaches epidemic stage. Character inspires character. Commitment begets commitment. Positive speech creates wholesome conversation.

Church is a contagious fellowship where we are continually infecting one another for righteousness in the spirit of Jesus. Isn't it encouraging to know that our best can be infectious? Would it not be sad to discover that the only thing about us that is contagious is our germs?

Virtues That Protect

Have you ever considered the virtues of the Christian life as antidotes to every evil that seeks to possess us? The protective power of goodness is strong motivation for pursuing the Godly life. Every detail of life's temptations is covered by the extraordinary influences of the righteous life.

For example, in the presence of hate there is love to sooth and heal our heated hostilities. As we struggle with doubt, there is the fact of faith to conquer our instability. In the face of fear we are confronted with courage that eliminates danger as a deterrent to the Godly life. Every ugly thought falters in its ambition to muddy our minds in the context of sober thinking. Despair is limited when hope is our daily companion. Lust is lost in the satisfying atmosphere of prayer. Pride is overcome by the humbling experiences that produce a gentle spirit.

Everywhere there is an evil; there is a virtue to combat it. The exciting fact here is God has not left us at the mercy of the devil. We have access to divine resources in our battle with sin. We do not have to succumb to the powers and principalities of this world. There is more to us than our evil inclinations. We are created sufficiently in the image of God to make our choice. "The devil made me do it" is no longer an alibi for misbehavior.

Even when evil overwhelms us and we sin, through confession and repentance we have the force of forgiveness to sustain us. As forgiven sinners we move through every evil situation by the virtues of God's grace. "Blessed are those who persevere under trial for they shall receive the crown of life." Amen

Polarities and Problems

Life is filled with many complicated issues. Chaos abounds. Trouble is everywhere. Evil has a way of creeping into any system we may have thought was immune to its tragic power. We cannot escape the perplexities of our times. For the most part we are locked into whatever circumstances surround us. Even church, which offers the saving grace of Jesus, is not free from the turmoil of confusion. We are in a world obsessed with selfishness, hopelessness and godliness. Despair is written on our faces. We are challenged to do the best we can with what we have as we find responsible ways to cope with life's agenda.

As we face the complicated issues of life we do well to distinguish between that which is a polarity and that which is a problem. Polarities are situations which have no clearly defined solution. They represent unresolvable difference s of opinions on each end of the mental spectrum. Issues, which are clearly non-negotiable, are polarities. People with extreme opinions tend to polarize themselves from the mainstream of human thought. It is well to understand that we only manage polarities. We do not solve them.

One of the ways we manage polarities is to look at the pluses and the minuses of each conflicting view. Here we need some consensus without compromise. We learn to disagree without becoming disagreeable. We coexist in the midst of our differences. On such issues our most helpful conclusion may be an admission that we have unresolvable polarities.

Problems, on the other hand, are situations, which are solvable with a reasonable amount of effort. We may not know the solution, yet we know the issues have reconciling possibilities. We delve into the dynamics of certain problems with the assurance something can be worked out. We apply the skills of diplomacy and pray for Godly wisdom. As God's spirit is allowed to work in our minds, stubbornness gives way to submission and darkness gives way to light. Forgiveness and grace rule over the problem until its solution is achieved. Of course a problem can become a polarity if we choose to exaggerate a certain

Let us, therefore, grow through the management of our polarities. We maintain our convictions; yet accept the reality of other opinions. We likewise pursue our problems with their solution as our goal. We invite God to make us "wise as serpents and harmless as doves." To understand this approach to life's complexities can be redemptive.

"Amazable"

A preschooler had just finished her first week ever of Vacation Bible School. Apparently it had been a good experience. When asked she told her mother "Vacation Bible School was amazable." Now adults may smile at the use of such a word, but to a child caught up in the excitement of learning about God it was a beautiful way to express it. She probably said more than she understood. Nonetheless, she found a way to describe a profound happening in her young life. How long has it been since you had an "amazable" event in your life? How long has it been since you needed to invent a word to describe something that ordinary words do not cover?

From time to time it is good to have an "amazable" experience. It is imperative that we have some blessed events come our way lest we become morbidly pessimistic. Life is filled with too many complicated issues. There is often mystery without meaning, problems without solutions, and heartache without comfort. Tragedy, sorrow, and death can take their toll upon us. As we move closer and closer to our final destiny we need some "amazable" things to cheer us on our way. It is not easy being human. Without some unexplainable joy overtaking us on the journey we could easily give up in hopeless despair.

Sometimes we may miss that which is "amazable." We turn a corner and there is God as big as life. If we fail to celebrate and share such an encounter it may have little or no effect upon us. The small light that shines into the darkness of our despair is better than no light at all. The more we focus upon it the brighter it glows to dispel the black that may surround us.

Friends who come our way in times of need may not overwhelm us, yet they are "amazable" in the way they can help heal our hurts. Sin may overtake us and guilt may unmercifully whip us, but grace is God's "amazable" reaction. He forgives the repentant and encourages the wayward to sin no more.

Love is an "Amazable" ingredient of life. The capacity to care and to be

Church and State

The Constitution of the United States guarantees the separation of church and state. This means that no body of believers, no religious sect nor any organized form of religion will have controlling influence in our government. It also means that the government will not grant special privileges to any religious group. The government will be neutral when it comes to making laws that might interfere with one's preference of faith and practice. In other words the government guarantees the freedom of religion, the freedom for religion and the freedom from religion.

Separation of church and state does not mean religious folk cannot have input into the process of government. Belief in God with all its ethical and moral implications for a civilized society is a duty we as Christians pledge to our land. Our convictions can be properly promoted as long as we are not abusive and destructive in the way we express them. We can vote for the kind of people who best represent our ideals, but once they are elected they cannot use their office to promote our style of religion. We do not lobby for laws that will advance our kind of church. We can lobby, however, for laws that will enhance a sense of decency and wellbeing in our country.

Our nation is in need of good and Godly citizens and government leaders who understand the Constitution and will not try to manipulate it to serve some private agenda. Our greatness as a nation has evolved from our willingness to recognize God's participation in the prosperity of our land. Patriotism and piety go hand in hand. Our commitment to both God and country gives strength to both. We love our country not more than God, but with Godly aspirations.

Patriotism does not mean our political leaders have no accountability to us. Democracy is a form of government where responsible protest can be made. In a government of the people, by the people and for the people we have a right and a duty to make a moral investment. No democratic government is any stronger than the quality of its people. Therefore, every honorable religious entity has a reason to sing "God Bless America." As we observe the religious oppression of other forms of government in our world we thank God and take courage in our own. We thank God for the freedom to pursue an authentic faith. We take courage in our ability to be a kind and gentle people.

Church Invaluable

In spite of adversaries and critics the church of our Lord Jesus Christ continues to have a redemptive role in contemporary society. In no way has modern technology diminished the need for this fellowship of faith. Although our procedures and programs may change, the gospel of grace has an unchanging appeal for all who need love and forgiveness. While church, by no stretch of the imagination, is a majority effort, it does have a healing effect upon the total community. Withdraw the church from society and there is a lost dimension of righteousness that is necessary for stability, productivity and progress.

Church at its best gives the Word of God priority and keeps the Lordship of Christ as a goal for its fellowship. In no way is there a perfect church. No one church can claim spiritual superiority over any other church. Hopefully, each church is a growing, repenting, struggling family of believers who have become church for the glory of God and the service of humankind.

As church we face the future keenly aware we have no future without Christ. "Our hope is built on nothing less than Jesus' blood and righteousness." The only way we can venture a dream about tomorrow is because we know who holds that tomorrow. We are secure in His promises and certain in His ability to be with us even to the end of the age. We move forward in faith not because we are so great, but because we serve a great God. Our future is in the hands of Him who said, "On this rock I will build my church and the gates of hell shall not prevail against it."

Therefore, we celebrate the church today as a people who are enjoying the spiritual benefits of our predecessors. Our real challenge is that we pass on this high and holy calling to all those who shall come after us. From the hands of our spiritual parents we reach forth a hand of hope to our spiritual children.

Personal Perspectives

Why?

It is a common human tendency to complain when we are faced with difficult circumstances. When things go wrong we are prone to ask "Why?" We want someone to give answers to the complicated issues of our lives. We want to blame someone for the hurt and misery our problems have created. Often it is God who is the recipient of our frustration. The mystery of misfortune leaves us with nothing but bitter confusion as to why God allows such pain. It is as though we believe God is the author of all our trouble.

Is it not strange that in adversity we are filled with questions, while we quietly accept our blessings? Surely there is as much mystery to life's good fortune as there is to life's tribulation. Yet, seldom do we ever hear someone puzzled about his or her well-being. Is it because we take life's rewards for granted? Do we subtly assume that we are entitled to reap the benefits of life's resources? Is God obligated to prosper us if we are good? What about the prosperity of those who are not good? Actually are any of us worthy of the happiness and blessings, which come our way?

Just as we cannot grasp the mystery of misfortune, we cannot solve the secret of good fortune. Grace is so amazing and so divine. Yet, it comes to us in physical as well as spiritual ways. May the sheer surprise of life's blessings find us grateful and humble. God forbid that we take pride in that which is not within our power to produce. "Every good gift cometh from above." We do well to ponder that mystery also.

Jealousy

Jealousy is a terrible curse on the human personality. It has a devastating effect upon our self-opinions. Jealousy arises out of a deep dissatisfaction with who we are and what we have. It keeps us searching endlessly for that which we think can make us complete. When we see what we think we want and someone else has it, we resent the fact that, somehow, life has denied us and favored another. It is a terrible way to live because we never know the joy of contentment.

A good relationship with others is often hindered because we are continually in competition with anyone who has what we want. Friendships are fractured at the slightest hint we are losing ground in the race to be "most successful." Fellowship with the Father is affected by our need to test His willingness to get us what we want. We often blame God for our lagging status, since our egos are ill equipped to accept any personal fault for our lot in life.

Jealousy is a subtle sin which, even if detected, we find difficult to confess. None of us want to admit we are jealous, yet it is one of our most obvious weaknesses. Because who we are, what we do, and what we have consumes so much of us, our jealousies cannot be completely hidden. They become a part of our personality as they determine the tone of our behavior.

We may think that jealousy is a minor flaw in our humanity, but in reality it furnishes much of the fuel for every sin in our lives. To honestly analyze our most devious iniquities is to discover the far-reaching effects of our jealous nature. Our only hope out of this jail of jealousy, in which we find ourselves incarcerated, is to seek the mind of Christ.

Our Lord taught us by word and deed that self-worth is determined more by what we give up than what we get. Once we move from self to sacrifice, jealousy loses much of its power over us. When our competitive spirits give way to a genuine hunger and thirst for righteousness, we lose our need to feel superior toward anyone.

The cross of Jesus becomes not only a symbol of our faith but a lesson on how to find our lives by losing them. Jealousy does not have to dominate our disposition if the servanthood of Jesus is our model. In the development of our own self-giving, we may learn to like ourselves enough to like those toward whom we may have been jealous.

Right and Wrong

Is it all right to be wrong? It is not, if we know what we are doing. "To him who knows to do right and does it not, to him it is a sin." It's not all right to be wrong when we deliberately disobey the will of God. It is not all right to violate the inner decency of our being. We will be held accountable for the way we bribe our conscience and mutilate our self-respect. It is not all right to be wrong if we know better.

It is all right to be wrong if we struggle in ignorance and make some wrong decisions as long as repentance and honesty prevail. It is all right not to know all the answers if our goal is to let God guide us to the truth. It is all right to admit our frailty. In fact, it may be the beginning of spiritual birth to acknowledge that sin is the culprit leading our lives toward defeat. It is all right to struggle with the issues of life and give God some growing room in our hearts.

Only those too right to ever be wrong are the ones who will never know the relief of confession and the joy of forgiveness. Only those for whom repentance is only a word and never a deed will have the emptiness of despair as a constant companion. It is disastrous to try to play God with such limited resources. Yes, it is all right to be wrong when we trust God for our righteousness.

It is all right to be human as long as we honor the image of God within. Is it all right to be wrong? Sometimes it is and it all depends on our capacity for grace. If we are willing to let God be God, we are equipped to let our weakness rest on His strength. Hallelujah what a Savior!

Anger

The energy of anger is a force to be reckoned with in our world. It can cause nation to rise against nation. It can cause neighbor to mistreat neighbor and families to crumble in pain. It can cause normally decent people to harbor hatred. It can cause all of us to lose our composure and make fools of ourselves.

What is there about this mysterious power, which causes us so much inner pain and frustration? Sometimes anger gains its strength from our exaggerated selfishness. It receives momentum from the "mighty me" complex. Anger preys on our weaknesses to make us feel strong. It makes us defensive and resentful toward those who detect the flaws in our armor. When we allow the sun to go down upon our wrath it complicates tomorrow's relationships.

Misdirected anger can be one of our most harmful emotions. Yet it does not always need to be bad. Paul said, "Be angry and sin not." Perhaps this is Paul's way of acknowledging a proper anger. It is a proper anger that runs moneychangers from the temple when it is obvious they are keeping others from worship. It is right to be angry about the hurts of life when they rise out of mistreatment and evil. Paul is telling us to channel the energy of our wrath into constructive purposes.

As the Holy Spirit controls our lives, even the emotion of anger becomes a redemptive tool in the hands of God. As our anger is kindled against sin, we are energized to oppose it. There are things God does not want us to tolerate. He wants us to despise the sin that separates us from one another. He wants us to denounce the evils, which destroy human personality.

Therefore, let us seek Him who can inspire us to be angry about sin and yet have love for the sinner. Let us be angry enough at sin to confess, repent, and turn from the awkward attitudes and actions, which have stunted our spiritual growth. Let us be angry enough at hate to let love prevail, at fear to let courage inspire, at doubt to let faith direct, and at

Joy

One of the intriguing aspects of our Christian commitment is the joy of belonging to Jesus. There is no way to minimize the underlying contentment of knowing we are in His care. The thrust of our spiritual excitement is rooted in the consciousness of God's involvement in our lives. From this holy exuberance we are motivated to go and to give as we participate in our Lord's commission. In many ways joy is the essence of our spiritual pilgrimage. It is the present benefit of our eternal hope. Joy equips us for the living of these days in anticipation of God's glorious future.

This does not mean that Christian joy removes all sadness and hurt from our hearts. It gives meaning to the grief, which we bear, and thus enables us to sorrow as those who have hope. We do not survive because we are immune to the pains and penalties of life. We survive because He who is in us is greater than he who is in the world. Our joy is a by-product of our struggle to live in the context of God's will. It is the peace and satisfaction, which comes from identifying with Him who is Lord of lords and King of kings forever and ever.

Genuine joy, however, cannot be synthetically produced. It is not derived from hyper-emotional religious ceremonies, which are temporarily exhilarating. Christian joy does not come by ignorantly sticking our heads in the sand and refusing to face life as it is. Jesus, the Lord of joy, leads us through life's hardships as well as happiness with the assurance that we are in good hands.

Our faith, which enables us to trust the eternal goodness of God, is the key to the kind of joy, which overcomes the world. No wonder that in Christ we know a joy that is unspeakable and a peace that passes all understanding. Believing that joy is possible in our kind of world makes us more than conquerors through Him who loves us through our times of despair. May you be blessed by the joy of reflecting on these words.

The Sheep Lesson

When the shepherd calls the sheep, they begin to gather around him, and there is a point at which the sheep cannot get closer to the shepherd without getting close to other sheep. Here is a law, which applies not only to physical space, but it is equally appropriate to spiritual fellowship. God calls us unto Himself as family. It is as brothers and sisters that we move into nearness with the heavenly Father. The group dynamics of being church is an awesome challenge to our patience and acceptance toward others. There is absolutely no way to get closer to God without getting closer to people who are equally called into the circle of His love.

When we find ourselves in intimate fellowship with Jesus, we will also discover the kind of people to whom He wishes to minister. There will be lepers and demoniacs, Pharisees and harlots, greedy tax collectors and sinners of every description. If we do not have the stomach to be around such "reprobates," we may never get near our Lord. It's not that our Lord condones unbecoming behavior. Those who are well do not need the Physician. Getting near to Jesus brings us into contact with people who are as good and as bad as we are.

Sometimes we avoid getting too close to Him because the pain of seeing ourselves in those humbled by His presence is too much for our spiritual pride. We remain a safe distance from Him in order to keep our distance from folk who have nothing to lose in giving their all to Jesus. Getting in there with all those sheep close to Jesus makes us vulnerable to such things as confession, repentance and a Godly lifestyle. Proximity to Jesus makes forgiveness and restoration a prerequisite for fellowship.

When we get close enough to Him to see how He treats all the sheep, we are moved to imitate His care. It is in our distance from Him that we feel free to let our hostility spill over into such things as Godless sarcasm, hateful criticism, unnecessary retaliation and unkindness of every description. In our distance, we think we can see well enough to judge one another.

In our closeness, however, we see that we are all so much alike we can find no one on whom to look down. Our so-called spiritual superiority

Affluenza

"Affluenza" is a make-believe word, which could describe an ailment, which afflicts us all at times. It could have its origin in the word, "affluence," which means the overabundance of material things. Of course, there is no such word in the dictionary but the condition still exists. We can easily become obsessed with the need to have things and perhaps more and better things than anyone else. We find ourselves addicted to prosperity in such exaggerated proportions that it affects our mental, emotional and spiritual well-being. Our diseased "wanters" create an unhealthy ambition, which has a devastating effect upon our physical stamina.

Perhaps there is no better way to describe this condition than to call it "affluenza." It is a disease, which has epidemic possibilities. "Affluenza" is highly contagious because it attacks our ego systems where greed, jealousy and snobbishness make us vulnerable to its infective power. Once the disease has invaded our need to feel important, we can no longer accept the prosperity of others. We develop a long list of folk we consider competitors because they have offended us by their affluency. We become locked into a disease, which is fed by an arrogant spirit.

Once the rat race begins, few if any folk have the courage to forfeit. It is a matter of pride even though our materialistic addiction spends us into bankruptcy. The economic structures of our society keep infecting us with "affluenza" in order to keep selling us things. We are gullible to the point of losing ourselves in an attempt to make an impressive display of what we do or do not have. It is so easy to become victims of our own fantasies and be caught in the web of our own ambitions.

The only cure for the exhaustion of "affluenza" is a commitment to Jesus who puts things in proper spiritual perspective. There is a spiritual dimension to prosperity, which honors God with our affluency. Humility as well as integrity builds up our immunity against "affluenza." When Jesus is truly Lord, our need to impress others is lost in a sense of servanthood. We no longer feel superior because we have more. We find meaning and joy in the fact that to whom much is given much is required. There is a stewardship about life, which cures our "affluenza" and adds greater value to everything we own. So, in everything we give thanks.

Doubt

Sometimes in the midst of our spiritual struggles we tend to be troubled with doubt. We doubt our salvation. We doubt the existence of God. We doubt our place in God's economy. It is a common occurrence among people who are sensitive to the pain of sin and the conviction of the Holy Spirit. It is not always as bad as it may seem, however, because doubt can be a means of stimulating our quest for the deeper life in Christ. The fact that we doubt could be an indication that our faith is authentic. Seldom if ever do we see disbelieving sinners worried about the validity of their experience in Christ. Godless people are not burdened with questions concerning their commitment to Christ.

It seems that doubt is the devil's tool to disturb a believing heart. Only those who are trusting Christ for salvation are vulnerable to the tricky questions of doubt. Only people with a serious nature about the things of God will worry about the caliber of their commitment.

Now please do not misunderstand. Doubt is not necessarily a virtue. It is a hindrance. Doubt is designed to weaken and frustrate as it creates a mood of pessimism and defeat. Carried to its logical conclusion, doubt destroys faith and stifles all spiritual initiative. While it is inspired by the enemy, when it is overcome it creates a closer walk with our Lord. It can be a springboard to challenge our best thinking. In honestly dealing with our doubts we soon discover in whom we have believed. Doubt is always on the diet and training table of healthy Christians who are learning to deny their doubts and affirm their faith. So "Have faith in God, He's on the throne."

A Miracle

A miracle is not a miracle until its source has been recognized and celebrated. A beautiful sunset loses much of its splendor without a grasp of Who causes it to happen. The dawning of a new day is a spectacular event for all who see the divine paintbrush at work. Life is dull and routine if there is no awareness of God's intervention in its particulars. Every day is full of mystery and meaning. The miraculous is as common as the explainable. The journey of life is one of faith. It requires us to see beyond the natural to the supernatural. Most of life is lived in the context of that which we do not fully understand. We simply trust the process observing much of which we consider is miraculous.

What then is a miracle? A miracle is any aspect of life that has God written all over it. It is not only that which is humanly unexplainable. It is that which has redemptive consequences for us. It is outside our ability to achieve. It is grace in motion as God's power to perform is recognized. A miracle is capable of many interpretations. All of us do not see the same miracles. They are individualized to minister to our unique circumstances. We must not minimize each other's miracles simply because we have a different interpretation to some event. Surely it would be a form of blasphemy to ridicule that which another person feels is God's involvement in his or her life.

We are blessed indeed when we can behold the hand of God at work in His world. When the miracles of life leap out at us in unexpected moments, we can surely praise God for His unmistakable presence. A miracle is not a miracle for us until we have some significant way to celebrate its occurrence. We do not announce every miracle as though we have a more favored position with God. A powerful personal miracle is a humbling experience and we savor the event only for God's glory. Sometimes it is a moment of grace for private interpretation only. Then again it may be an occasion for others to join the celebration. Let us be mindful of life's miracles and find ways to share God's power for God's glory.

A Closed Mind

There is a terrible tendency among most of us to assume that we are always right on every issue. We give little, if any, attention to another opinion because of our dogmatic commitment to our own ideas.

We are inflexible toward those with whom we disagree and sometimes suspicious of those with whom we agree. We often refuse to study the facts for fear we might have to change our position. The truth of the matter is that sometimes we even manipulate the facts to fit our own conclusions. We tie our ears to no voice except that which confirms our own prejudices. We close our minds on every topic and, in so doing; we shut out the Holy Spirit who enables us to grow in truth and grace.

It is a tragic predicament of our souls to lose our ability to consider another way or another idea and change if and when change is required. The whole concept of repentance is based on the fact that we can change our minds and our ways. To be a disciple is to be a learner. To have a learning disposition is to be open to God-inspired truth wherever it may lead. The most pressing problem for our Lord's earthly ministry was a religious community ill-equipped to accept His Messianic changes. The rut of ritualism and a lamentable legalism combined to hinder the possibility of salvation for the Jews.

Truth continues to be a painful pursuit, even in our day. When we get set in our ways and opinions, it is hard to open our minds to the Holy Spirit as He leads us into new and exciting ventures of faith. No doubt the greatest hindrance to our own personal growth is a lack of openness to all God's truth. Such inflexibility of thought is a subtle humanism, which borders on the worship of our own mentality. Life is too big and our minds are too frail for us to rely only on our own perspectives. The holy inspired Bible is our greatest resource for studying all God would have us know. Let us not forsake its capacity to break us, mold us, and turn us in openness toward God.

Motive

Motive is a strange, yet significant energy within our lives. It is the power of our personality. It is the driving force of our ambition. It is the reason why we do what we do, say what we say and are who we are. Nothing moves us like our motives. It is important, therefore, to understand our motives if we are to understand ourselves. This is not always easy because often our motives are subtly camouflaged so that we do not honestly know why we do what we do, say what we say and are who we are. Sometimes our motives are clear and pure, while at other times they are fuzzy and ulterior. The fact that we do religious things does not always mean we have high religious motives.

Jesus, who looks deep within us, once observed that everyone who says, "Lord, Lord," will not enter the kingdom of heaven. He often verbally chastised scribes and Pharisees for making a spiritual appearance so as to attract human attention. The motive for prayer is best expressed in a closet where a desire for public praise does not distract. The motive for benevolence is always weak when excessive attention is called to the gift. Jesus cut through the rules and regulations of traditional religion and focused on the reality of God's revelation. He taught His disciples to examine their motives in the light of God's loving purpose and not their own self-interest.

The call to deny oneself is a demanding discipline. It is embarrassing and painful to discover how much of what we do, what we say and who we are is a subtle promotion of our own ego. Our praise, our prayers and our proclamation can easily become an occasion to call attention to ourselves. We cannot seem to escape the fact that we have a terrible need to be noticed. Yet, we must not allow this need to keep us from serving the Lord. He who calmed the boisterous waves can subdue the selfish uprising of our souls. He can use a strong ego for His glory and give us insight into our personalities, which will produce a humble disposition. To know He loves us, as we are, inspires us to evaluate why we do what we do, say what we say and are who we are.

Our motives will never be entirely pure as long as we contend with our human limitations, but we do not have to surrender. Whatever drives us can drive us to seek Godly goals and serve righteous purposes however imperfect our vision may be. When Jesus said, "Blessed are the pure in heart", He was commending those who allow themselves to be motivated by a desire to please God. Why then do we do what we do, say what we say and are who we are? Our struggle with this question will go a long way in purifying our motives.

Escape the Gloom

Sadness is a strange and awkward companion that travels with all of us from time to time. It attaches itself to us with devastating effects upon our outward appearance. Our somber countenance is a dead giveaway that we have been invaded by an unhappy circumstance. We cannot always hide the mood of sadness behind artificial smiles and forced optimism. It cuts deep into the heart of who we are and eventually affects everything we say and do.

Sadness is the culprit that causes us to miss out on life's happiest moments. It takes over our emotions and completely immobilizes our ability to laugh. How sad when sorrow and despair become the dominant ingredients of our otherwise happy disposition. Life loses some of its meaning when our mood is one of melancholy. Hope struggles to survive and joy is shattered when gloom takes over.

We live in a day that spreads sadness with ever increasing effectiveness. We are inundated with news that focuses upon the tragic, the destructive, and the evil aspects of our society. As a population of people drawn to the bizarre and the unusual, we seem to thrive more on bad new than on good news. Bad news tends to be more dramatic while good news seems tame and uneventful. Shock and horror are the things that get our adrenalin flowing.

No wonder we are basically a sad society. Our steady diet of gloomy information makes a demoralizing contribution to the unhealthiness and unhappiness of our inner being. No wonder drugs and alcohol are used in excess. It is the only way some folk feel they can cope with the deep, deep sadness of their soul.

Others of us have any number of ways to escape the feelings of loneliness that grip our souls. We work ourselves to exhaustion. We play ourselves silly. We travel ourselves dizzy. All of this and more, simply to escape the trail of sadness that follows us like a plague.

Our greatest need, however, is not escape, but a legitimate way to resolve our inner gloom. Simon Peter comes to our rescue by advising us to cast all our anxiety on Jesus because He cares for us. The hymn writer tells us to "take it to the Lord in prayer." He who was a man of sorrow and acquainted with grief understands the depth of our sadness. We can spread our stories of despair before Him, no matter how awkwardly expressed, and know He cares for us.

No sadness is too trite and no grief is too exaggerated that our Lord will not hear us. There is no fear of rejection because our Lord Himself extends the invitation by saying, "Come unto me, all you who labor and are heavy laden, and I will give you rest."

Silver or Rusty Spoons

Some people come into the world with a tremendous financial advantage. Their forebears have provided them with substantial resources. Some of them make the most of it and live productive lives. Others squander their inheritance by reckless mismanagement. It is no crime to enter into life with a prosperous endowment. There is nothing wrong in having one's life fully funded. It is a sin, however, to abuse one's advantage. "To whom much has been given much is required." There is a stewardship of life that expects us to do the best we can with what we have. There is such a thing as responsible abundance. Affluent folk are uniquely blessed with many avenues of special service to humankind. No matter what our status at birth we all have a lifetime to establish our worth.

We sometimes refer to people entering life with an abundance of material resources as having been born "with silver spoons in their mouths." Perhaps many of us feel as if we were born with rusty spoons in our mouths. We certainly brought nothing into the world. We had little offered us on arrival and we are leaving very little behind in terms of material wealth. Nonetheless, we are trying to do the best we can with what we have. Whatever good, whatever bad, whatever rich, whatever poor, whatever great, and whatever small there is about us, we are primarily responsible.

The kind of spoon with which we were born need not determine the quality of our contribution. Just as it is no crime to be rich, it is no crime to be poor unless our poverty is a poverty of soul. God has created us with the freedom to be the best we can be with the set of circumstances life has imposed upon us. He does not require us to build a financial fortune. He expects us to be fruitful and multiply. He wants the spot we inhabit on planet earth to be productive. God desires that we use our creative energies in positive ways.

Whether we come into the world with a silver spoon or a rusty spoon we still have a purpose. We start from where we are and move to where we can be by the grace of God. Neither riches nor poverty is an excuse for lazy living. We take hold of that bit of life we have been given and pursue the richness of God's possibilities for us. Our investment is called "commitment." The return is called "contentment." No matter what kind of spoon from which we eat, we are either nourished or impoverished by what we digest.

The Christian Advantage

What is our advantage as Christians? Do we have a special protection from the pains and penalties of life? Is ours a special standing before God as though He gives us favored treatment? Are we somehow exempt from war, pestilence, famine and disease? The answer is "no" because life does not seem to have favorites. It tends to rain misfortune and blessings upon the just as well as the unjust. We do have an advantage as Christian, however, and our advantage is that in the midst of tribulation, distress, persecution, famine, nakedness, peril, or sword we are more than conquerors. God meets us in the rut of our own agonies to show us who we are. He inspires our perseverance. He tutors us through our trauma. He gives us a reason to believe in ourselves and those who meet us in the valley of our tears. He magnifies the meaning of grace even though healing might never happen.

Our advantage is not some mysterious rescue. It is a powerful Presence from which there is no separation. Paul reminds us that none of the troublesome things of life can ever separate us from the love of God in Christ Jesus. In fact we are not exempt from them. We are blessed through them. Sometimes it takes these things to help us discover the love we have. Even though most times we make the very hell we live in, He wants to meet us in the lowest moments of our lives. Whatever disease and despair may wish to conquer us, He reminds us that we are not far from Him.

Of course there are times when God appears to be silent and absent. Our prayers for a "quick fix" or a dramatic intervention seem to fall on deaf ears. Our childish concept of a God who will rescue us in every difficulty disappoints us. We want to shake our fist at God and cry, "unfair, unfair!" But then in the midst of our most painful moment we discover a peace that is unexplainable. We find an unconquerable reason for faith and hope. We experience a grave-defying assurance that even the "valley of the shadow of death" is crossable. It is as though our most troubling moments usher us into a meeting place with God. No, He does not put us there. He finds us there and we are conditioned to receive Him there. Our advantage is simply this...nothing, and that means nothing, can separate us from the love of God. Faith connects us to that kind of hope.

Memories

One of the significant features of life as we grow older is a set of dear memories, which we establish along the way. Our minds have a marvelous capacity to store sweet relationships and special events where love and happiness prevailed. It is indeed an act of grace to be able to recall those beautiful moments and celebrate the goodness of God. Worship is enhanced by memory, which allows us to focus our attention on the One from whom all blessings flow. Of a truth God is the author of our dear memories as He leads us to people, places and events of unforgettable consequences.

Of course memory can be painful and harsh if the quality of our relationships have been characterized by nagging neglect. In no way can we draw rich dividends from our memory banks unless along the way we make some significant deposits. We cannot ignore the fact that how we live today greatly affects our happiness tomorrow. We are all in the process of building some memories and how blessed we will be in years to come if we can look back and call them "precious."

Do not despair, however, if your memories are sad. In love God calls us to remember, to repent and to start a whole new set of memories. In the context of His grace he gives us a place to begin again. When memories are sad and life has lost its zest, God gives us a reason to remember our hope. It is the Lord Jesus our Savior who says, "This do in remembrance of Me." How blessed we are today to be able to invest in some future memories of notable quality.

Confidence

Confidence is a serious item on the chart of our personality needs. It contributes to our productivity by giving us a wholesome sense of self-worth. Confidence enables us to feel secure in what we are able to say and do. It is the ability to believe in ourselves even when others may doubt our potential. Without confidence we lose the pep of our personality. We lose the inner strength to project an outgoing disposition. As we develop a sagging self-image we lack the willpower to succeed. It is a tragic waste of spiritual and mental energy when we lose our confidence. We can never be all God wants us to be if our composure is limited.

Confidence is the product of our faith. It begins with a strong belief that God is in us to work His will and purpose. We take our cue from Paul who said, "I can do all things through Christ who strengthens me." With the backing of the Holy Spirit we have confidence that all things can work for good if we love God. Sometimes fear is a deterrent to our confidence. It causes us to focus on our weaknesses rather than our strengths. The psalmist comes to our rescue by reminding us that "the Lord is our light and our salvation whom shall we fear? The Lord is the stronghold of our lives of whom shall we be afraid?" This kind of faith in God is the basis of a confident commitment.

Faith in others is likewise a prerequisite for healthy confidence. Our ability to believe in someone else enhances our ability to believe in ourselves. Mistrust and doubt are the result of a poor self-image. To find folk who are stable and trustworthy is to find models for our own self-confidence. On the other hand, people who are nervous and insecure will rob us of our optimistic spirit. We must not give people the power to take away our confidence. As we seek the best in others and find the best in ourselves, we develop a fellowship of confident personalities.

Furthermore, faith in ourselves is the bottom line of our confidence. It gives us the energy and the courage to reach our potential. Believing that we can produce and survive amid the intimidating factors of life is necessary for our confidence. This does not mean we will always succeed. It means that failure will not have the last word. We accept God's grace and humbly develop self-forgiveness with confidence. We trust God and the positive encouragement of our friends to boost our morale and give us a confident spirit.

Forgiveness

Forgiveness is one of the most difficult aspects of our Christian behavior. It demands much from us in terms of compassion and grace. It stretches our human capacity for love to an unbelievable dimension. Sometimes it seems as if we are ill equipped to truly forgive those who are offensive. We want some kind of retribution against anyone who disturbs us by their ways or their thoughts. Often that which we think is forgiveness is nothing but a mild indifference or a condescending attitude toward those who sin against us. The burning rage is still there just beneath the surface and will burst into the flames of anger at the slightest provocation.

To honestly forgive is to develop a relationship and an attitude toward offending persons as if the offense never occurred. Since we are not conditioned to quickly forget, we have a problem with memory. We store a lot of sin in our memory, which inhibits our ability to forgive. The ministry of forgiveness, however, is our most potent Christian witness. Reaching out with kindness and grace toward those who have hurt us is our most God-like disposition.

While forgiveness is indeed a blessing upon those to whom we express it, there is also a deep personal benefit to us. The weight of revenge and hostility is baggage we do not need to carry. Our emotional and spiritual health require us to practice the discipline of reconciliation. Perhaps this is why our forgiveness toward others is vitally related to the kind of forgiveness we can experience from God.

An unforgiving spirit can never have much in common with the pardoning grace of God. There is a sense in which forgiveness begets forgiveness. Forgiveness, which we receive from others and from God, prepares us to express forgiveness. By experiencing grace, we are conditioned to be graceful. The humble recognition of our own need to repent of our sins and seek the favor of God as well as others teaches us the value of forgiving "those who trespass against us." How well do

Learning to Like Ourselves

Have you ever wondered why some people do not like you? No matter what you do or do not do, they find you rather repulsive. Since it is a normal tendency to want people to like us, we often grieve when dislike is obvious. Our frustrations are compounded when, to us, there are no apparent reasons for their rejection. It hurts to feel the hate of others when, in our hearts, we know it is not our intention to hurt anyone. If we are people who provoke conflict, then we can expect some "eye for an eye" reactions. But if, in the sincerity of our souls, we promote peace, then it is strange when others do not respond peaceably to us.

It seems that some folk need a few people toward whom they have an adversarial relationship, and at times we become their victims. It may be that we remind them of someone who hurt them in the past. It may be that we did not have the same opinion on some issue, and some people have tender egos when it comes to disagreement. Perhaps we do not share the same enemies, and that creates problems for folk with hostile attitudes. Again, it may be that we are perceived as being different and for some; conformity is a "religion." There are a variety of ways to analyze the dynamics of people's dislike of us for no apparent reasons.

Our healthiest response, however, is not analysis but confidence. Perhaps we need to learn to like ourselves. If to our own selves we have been true, we must never allow the disapproval of uncomplimentary folk to distract us from life's pursuit of happiness and purpose. Our strength can be the strength of ten if our hearts are pure. No one can ultimately defeat us unless we allow then to do so. In Christ we can do all things, as Paul would remind us.

We must humbly accept the fact that everyone is not going to like us. Our task as Christians is to make sure we do not give anyone legitimate reasons for their dislike. When there are offenses, as surely there will be, there must be the grace of apology and forgiveness. Turning the other cheek and going the second mile and returning good for evil help us to survive the most hostile environments.

There is a sense, however, in which we must not nervously try to please everyone; else we become moral and spiritual jellyfish. We take our stands, live life to its fullest and let God be God. Without offending people it is important to know in Whom we have believed and why. There is surely something to be learned from our Lord when He told His disciples to beware "when all men speak well of you."

Perception

Perception is a valuable part of our reasoning process. It equips us to comprehend some things without being told. It is the ability to sense the atmosphere of an occasion and to make proper responses. It is insight into a set of circumstances, which requires our best thinking. Perception is the art of forming opinions and making evaluations based on what we believe to be the truth.

The problem is that sometimes perception and reality are not the same. Because of our human limitations, we are quite capable of jumping to conclusions, which are unfounded. How often have we all formed opinions and made comments on the basis of what we thought was obvious only to learn later we had been mistaken? For this reason, we have to constantly monitor our perception to make sure that which we perceive is consistent with that which is. This is not an easy assignment, even for people of integrity, because we live in a world of confusing information.

Public perception is often marred by the mismanagement of facts. Rumor and misinformation get mistaken for the truth. This is why we must continually repent, rethink and recommit ourselves to him who is the way, the truth and the life. Only in Christ Jesus can our perceptions be accurate and our opinions Godly. Only in Him, who strongly advised us not to be judgmental, can we make evaluations that are redeeming. Through prayer and deep devotional activity, we are able to distinguish between wholesome perception and unfounded suspicion.

If indeed God has given us the gift of perception, it is not for us to be super-pious and critical, but to be intercessory in our relationship to others. What goes around usually comes around. Sooner or later we are all going to need the caring skills of others to help heal the wounds of our own lives. Our most healthy prayer may be, "Lord, I honestly believe, help me now to properly perceive. May the words of my mouth never betray the confession of my heart that you are Lord of lords and King of kings forever."

Hunger for the New

Do you ever feel a compulsion for something which is new? Are you so fearful of growing stale that you will accept most anything for a change? As searching Christians it is easy to get caught up in the current trends of religious thought. In an attempt to escape the dullness of our daily devotions, it is possible to become enamored by the latest theological fads. There are some folk who are always promoting a new way, a new voice and a new excitement to stimulate our sagging spiritual development. This is not all bad if it is centered in Christ Jesus and has the Holy Spirit as its guiding impetus.

If our commitment, however, is simply to something new, the novelty will soon wear off and our new enthusiasm will soon wither away. Sometimes it is not what is new that we need to learn. It is what we have forgotten that we need to remember. God is forever calling us back to the old paths and reminding us of the basics in discipleship and worship.

Let us never forget that faith must be the forerunner of our feelings. Real enthusiasm emerges from a strong belief in an exciting God. We must remember that honest prayer keeps us close to the voice of God. There is no short cut to intercession and communion with the Father. We must remember that God's word has a way of clarifying our theology. The Bible can add a lot of insight to our religious library.

Let us never forget that the sweet spirit of Jesus is still the model for our lives. New fads that might lead us to fight and quarrel over who are the "best" Christians are surely rooted in a contentious spirit. We keep the fact before us that the church is as old as our Lord's commission and while it will always need renewal and new challenges, it still offers us the age-old fellowship of redemption.

Therefore, let us make sure that the "new" for which we hunger is rooted in the "old" which has been trusted and tried. It is possible for the old time religion to have a new time appeal. However, if there is monotony in our ministry, the dullness is ours, not God's.

Know Thyself

Self-evaluation is a process that goes on within us with daily regularity. It's not so much a checklist of items, which gives us a reading on how we are doing. It is a subtle personal appraisal of everything we do and say. It is part of our self-image, which monitors our standing with others as well as with God. Even though we are not always conscious of it the process goes on. We are constantly making judgments as to whether or not we are equal to given situations. Consciously or subconsciously, we evaluate our performance in every area of life, and as we do we need to avoid two extremes.

First, we should avoid being excessively lenient in our self-appraisals. It is easy to see ourselves as better than we really are. We must avoid becoming cocky and overconfident so that we overpower others with a sense of our own self-importance. Nothing weakens our witness as a Christian like an assumption of spiritual superiority. It is interesting how we can look on the faults and failures of others as serious character flaws and yet minimize our own discrepancies. Just because our sins are different does not ever mean they are any less evil in the sight of God. It behooves us to look at ourselves honestly and realistically.

On the other hand, we must avoid the extreme of being too hard on ourselves. It is easy to think of our sins as worse than anyone else has ever committed. We look at other people and think they would never have our kind of thoughts or do our kind of sins. We assume we are some kind of sinful oddity, forgetting the Bible says, "We have had no temptation to confront us, but such is common to man."

Never learning how to lay our sins on Jesus, we desperately try to carry the whole load. Perhaps this is why we like the gossip circuit. We find some sordid satisfaction in learning about others whose sins are as bad as or worse than ours. We long for someone we can look down on. We try to prop up our low self-esteem by running other people down. This does not lessen our load, but adds to our accumulating guilt. The devil always wins when we allow sin to give us a spiritual inferiority complex.

The truth of the matter is that our sins are no worse nor better than those of others. From God's perspective we gain no advantage nor disadvantage in comparing iniquities. No matter how evil and devious our transgression we have not sinned past our ability to call upon God. It may be from the pit of ugliness that we look up and live. In confession there is relief. In repentance there is hope. In Christ there is grace, which is our best resource in knowing how we are doing.

For the Loving God

One of the most obvious requirements of the Christian life is that we love God. From the beginning of time it seems evident that God created us in His own image to love us and in turn be loved by us. Yet, the most piercing question is, how do we love God? What does it mean to love God with all our heart, mind, soul and being? How do we know we are loving God to the best of our ability? These are questions we need to ponder because they are at the heart of what it means to be a Christian person. So, how do we love God? Let us count the ways. By our feelings, our thoughts, and our actions we can determine the quality of our God-love.

Since we are emotional beings we are equipped to feel the presence of God. There will be occasions when we will deeply sense His goodness and grace. His comforting assurance will guide us through difficult situations. We will be impressed by things too wonderful to explain. There will be times when the beauty of creation and the evidence of divine handiwork will overwhelm us. At such times we will celebrate our existence. The fact that we are alive and aware of life's privileges and responsibilities gives us a reason to praise God. It may express itself with tears or laughter. Deep down, however, where words do not reach we know we love God.

We are also intelligent beings capable of thinking God's thoughts after Him. Our involvement with God includes our minds. Our faith commitment is cerebral. We are admonished to study and meditate upon the deeper things of God. Shallow thinking leads to superstition and fear. Integrity of thought leads us to the truth that sets us free. When the light bulbs of learning God's will and ways are turned on in our minds we celebrate His revelations. As our knowledge increases we discover how much we really love God with all our minds.

Perhaps the hardest expression of our love for God is in our actions. It is difficult at times to put our deep feelings and thoughts into our daily behavior. We feel and know far more than we do. Our strong emotional and mental attachment to God does not always find expression in the way we treat our neighbor. When it does, however, there is a completeness to our love for God, which blesses us with great satisfaction. When our walk, walks the talk then our love for God is working.

Thus we conclude that love for God is not one-dimensional. It is more than emotional spasms, intellectual gymnastics, or outward acts of superficial piety. Authentic love for God comes when every aspect of our being harmonizes in singing "My Jesus, I love Thee, I know Thou art mine."

Heart Trouble

The latch on the door of her heart was firmly fastened. There were years of disappointment kept tightly secured within her inner being. Memories were too painful to mess with. She punished herself daily for the sins of her past. Some were her own and some belonged to others. In a sordid kind of way she clung to her weaknesses as an excuse for being a loner. She rejected most people because of the mistreatment by a few. She respected no one because she had little respect for herself. It was too risky to have close friends who might try to pry open the door to her heart.

She was a beautiful person, but she did not know it. She constantly guarded the unacceptable person she thought was hiding somewhere within her subconscious. She would not let light shine into the dark cellar of her own self-image. The mistruths and mistreatments of others caused her to doubt her own sanity. She internalized everyone's behavior and at times enjoyed the role of martyr. Her door was shut and sealed, but the Savior kept knocking and saying, "Behold I stand at the door and knock. If you will open, I will come in and eat with you."

He was a macho man. The door to his heart was also closed. He enjoyed the male role in life. He took pride in his manliness, but it was a front. Deep inside he was afraid and lonely. He too had been hurt, but he was too "brave" to admit it. He could not afford to let others think there were cracks in his armor. When he allowed himself to cry (in total privacy) he was ashamed of his weakness. The need to be in control caused him to boast. The need always to be right made him defensive. He needed to talk to someone, but who would understand? There was a little boy inside who needed to escape, but he would not release him.

People looked up to him because they thought he was someone he was not. He looked down on himself because he knew he was not who they thought he was. Underneath his macho exterior was a kind and gentle person, but he would not let himself see this. The door to his heart was barricaded by many misconceptions of real manhood. The Savior kept knocking and saying, "Behold I stand at the door and knock. If you will open, I will come in and eat with you."

Stop! Listen! There may be Someone at the door of your heart. It is Jesus and He understands you better than you understand yourself. He is the only One who needs to come into your inner sanctum. You can confide in Him. He wants to come in, but the latch of your door is on the inside.

Being Oneself

There is an awesome beauty about people who do not have to prove their worth. There is a refreshing integrity from those who are content to be themselves. There is a wholesome fellowship with folk who are not on ego trips and feel no need to crush others by their superior speech or activity. It is a powerful attribute to be able to accept God's design for one's life without trying to redesign it. There is something to be said for those who have found God's will for their lives and are content to be a servant people.

Trying to be someone we are not is a frustration of great magnitude. It is a sin against God who made us the way we are for a reason. It is a source of contention with everyone we know because of the competitive nature of every relationship. The need to conquer and emerge to the top in every situation is the product of a poor self-image. In the long run it is not healthy to always have our own way. It creates a self-centeredness from which we tend to dominate others and multiplies our need to be "king of the mountain."

Servant people will always have occasions where they must decrease in order that others might increase. This can be done when there is a healthy understanding of who we are, especially who we are in Christ Jesus. God is forever calling us to accept ourselves as we are and grow by His grace into the beautiful people He has designed. Jesus has freely told us who we are. We are the salt of the earth and the light of the world. Let us, therefore, go forth to preserve and to guide with nothing to prove and nothing to lose.

Personal Hostility

One of the complicated realities of life is that we live in a world of much anger. Reading letters to editors in newspapers and magazines reveals a strong sense of hostility in those who write. Private conversation on certain topics can provoke heated discussion even among friends. Sometimes sermons and religious rhetoric contain an unusual amount of anger. Opinionated people are everywhere, ready to lash out at someone or some circumstance at the slightest provocation. There seems to be in many of us an inner rage that goes beyond the expression of strong convictions. The need to insult, embarrass and intimidate appears to be our most satisfying approach to any person with whom we disagree.

What is the source of this inner wrath which threatens both our happiness and our health? Is it an anger against parents and unresolved childhood frustrations? Does marital contention create a negative disposition toward life? Are we unfulfilled in our occupational pursuits? Is anger the only way we know to express displeasure? Are we mad at God and take it out on the rest of the world? We do well to monitor the level of our hostility and the reasons for it.

Most of us are unaware of this tension just under the surface of our otherwise pleasant dispositions. Often, the recipients of our angry outbursts are not the ones to whom our deeper hostilities are directed. The potential for conflict is ever present because we never know when something or someone will trigger our anger button. When it happens, we say and do things in haste, which tend to complicate the way we relate to one another. Here is where sin takes advantage of hostile feelings to create guilt and anxiety.

Our Lord, however, has not left us in a climate of contention with no hope. We do not have to surrender to the rage within or without. We can confess our faults to one another. We can forgive even as Christ has forgiven us. We can turn the other cheek and go the second mile. We can help each other with our personal hostilities. We can channel the learn to manage our moments of wrath. There is grace to deal with the inner rage that afflicts our society. Perhaps it begins with a love that recognizes and reaches out to a hurting humanity. In Christ we lose our reasons to be angry at anybody or anything.

Finding Our Potential

Sometimes we feel as if much of life is a waste of time. There is so much that is lost amid our many preoccupations. It seems impossible to make every moment count. We procrastinate. We daydream and we "while away" the time. So little of our attention is directed toward things that really matter. So often our focus is diverted to that which is peripheral and inconsequential. There is so much to do, and we do not have the time and energy to do it. There is so much to say and not enough words to say it. Where will we find the will to be all we are capable of being? Where is the heart for the difficult task and the perseverance for the weary journey?

It is easy to give up when our vision exceeds our resources. Discouragement sets in when we see so much and accomplish so little. Often it is the cause for doing nothing. Why should we spin our wheels and never make progress toward our destination? If we cannot do everything, why do anything? Failure comes in different packages. Sometimes it is an over exaggerated ambition. We lose ourselves before we get started. We bite off more than we can chew. We focus on the finishing before we have prepared for the beginning. Too much ambition can be as bad as no ambition. Often the results are the same.

What then is our potential? Our greatest achievements may not come in trying to do everything, but in doing a few things well. Our greatest lessons may be in learning our weaknesses as well as our strengths. The ability to accept our limitations may equip us to highlight our possibilities. No one can be best at everything. Everyone can enjoy being who they are and how their gifts define them. Life is too short to be frustrated by the impossible. It is long enough, however, to pursue the possible and celebrate the joy of doing our best.

We are blessed indeed when we find the power to persevere at the level of our personal performance. Our most depressing sin is trying to do more than or less than the level of our potential. Our most promising virtue is to work and to put our work in perspective as we leave the rest

Close Minds, Hard Hearts

People who are dogmatically sure that they are always right are a hindrance to the cause of Christ. A "bulldog" commitment to some cause or system of thought leads to any number of evils. Folk with an exaggerated zeal for their position will lie, steal, loot, burn or even kill for their understanding of how life is put together. It is the old principle that the end justifies the means. Religion is no exception to such extremism. Many things have been done in the name of Christ but are completely out of character with the spirit of Christ. It matters not how worthy our cause, if we use the devil's methods to achieve it, then the devil wins. He doesn't care how sanctimonious and pious we may sound, if he can only give us a hateful approach to our convictions. The devil thrives on people who worship their perception of God rather than God Himself. It is essential to have convictions and principles as a basis for putting our lives together. It is harmful, however, when our convictions and principles become rigid and self-serving. When they become more important to us than people or even God, we are in danger of developing a loveless legalism.

It might be well for us, at times, to have a healthy suspicion that we could be wrong on some things. To consider the possibility that there are other ways of seeing things gives us a gentler disposition toward those with whom we may disagree. Being open and receptive to the Holy Spirit means God has other things for us to consider. He wants us to be teachable and flexible to His leadership in every circumstance. Growing in the grace and knowledge of our Lord Jesus implies that we have not learned it all. As a follower of Jesus, we are not on a dead-end street to the back alleys of a hopeless hypocrisy. We are on an open highway where life's possibilities are as big as heaven itself.

When we close our minds, we harden our hearts and we lose the compassion we are called to express. Being stable and theologically sound is much more than protecting our own prejudices. It is a humble attempt to understand what "thus saith the Lord" and then seek to apply His special word in every situation. Life is far too complicated for us to live it without a Savior and a Helper. When love is the motive of our lives, the grace of our Lord and the guidance of the Holy Spirit will keep us from worshipping at the shrine of our own opinion.

Good Guilt

Guilt is a topic, which quickly claims our attention because of the feeling of shame with which we struggle. When the subject is addressed we listen intently in hope someone can somehow explain why we feel badly about ourselves. What is this inner urging, which keeps us constantly, dissatisfied with our behavior? Where does the voice come from that sometimes shouts "shame, shame"? Is there no relief from the annoying pain of who we are? The answer is yes. Biblical faith and salvation history focus upon the fact that we do not have to stay the way we are. The whole concept of God's atonement is that we lay our sins on Jesus. In doing so we do not become sinless, but we are forgiven. Our guilt is resolved in confession and faith.

The spiritual benefit of our guilt is in its ability to monitor any behavior that does not conform to our code of conduct in Christ. Hopefully the church, the scriptures and family training have given us a healthy sensitivity to the mind of Christ. If permitted, the Holy Spirit will give us a Godly disposition in the way we think and act. When we quench the Spirit and violate the will of God there is a holy discomfort. The anticipation of pain caused by our transgressions is a deterrent to reckless living.

There is indeed a good guilt. Our conscience, if properly nurtured, can be our most helpful companion in our attempt to walk "the straight and narrow." Guilt can be good for us if it motivates us to correct our mistakes and improve our relationships. If it leads us to repentance and restoration then we have benefited from whatever pain it may have produced. When we can transgress and feel no pain we are indeed dead in our "trespasses and sins."

On the other hand, however, guilt can become a hindrance to our happiness when there are no channels of confession through which it may flow from our burdened souls. Morbid guilt is a preoccupation with our sin rather than a humble appeal for pardoning grace. It can produce an unhealthy grief for the sins we are too weak to avoid. Guilt can drag

Responding to Despair

Deep within the valley of despair, we are often conditioned to find the green pastures of spiritual nourishment and the still waters of God's grace. Perhaps we are never nearer God than when our hearts are heavy and our mental resources seem exhausted. Too often, in the proud world of our own achievements, we develop an arrogance, which denies the need for faith. In the mirror of our own self-importance, we fail to see the image of God in which we were created.

How blessed we are when circumstances crush our haughty spirits and give us a realistic picture of ourselves and our world. Although God does not cause our moments of depression, He is prepared to use them for our growth. With whatever it takes to get our attention, God is ready to lead us on the journey of grace. Our most profound thoughts and invigorating insights are not the product of frivolity. It is in the serious and solemn reaction to life's burdens, we seek the mind of Christ.

We are conditioned to think God's thoughts only when we recognize our desperate need for divine perspective. In humble recognition of our own inadequacies we place our hand in the nail-scarred hand of Jesus. From His submission to the Father, we learn the significance of our own surrender. In His pain, we see the redemptive value of our own suffering. In many ways, we see a cross running through the complexity of life. Sooner or later, we all face denial, betrayal and crucifixion of one kind or another. Life has a variety of ways of imposing its penalties upon us.

Our greatest response is to accept adversity as an opportunity to be creative and flexible. God has equipped us with a capacity to deal with life's obstacles. Of course, there will be times when despondency and despair are inevitable. These moments need not be devastating, however, if we see them as a part of God's humbling process where submission and trust begin. Our somber meditation may be a time of greater learning, which leads to greater joy.

Integrity

Integrity is a virtue, which has multiple possibilities for our well-being. It is the heart and soul of our moral and spiritual capabilities. Integrity gives direction to our lives as we commit ourselves to the many facets of truth, which affect us. Integrity includes, but is more than, simply telling the truth. It is a dedication to all that is honorable and honest in life. With integrity, we do not sell our souls to the highest bidder. With integrity, we experience freedom from the restricting power of pretense. We lose the need to be mere play actors in the drama of life. We become real live participants in the kingdom of God.

Our Lord's most ambitious dream while on earth was to restore integrity to organized religion. In attempting to do so it cost Him his life. Integrity can be a demanding taskmaster. It can create an atmosphere of anxiety and pain. Yet, it paves the way for authentic servanthood. Jesus left us a legacy of truth, which is our model.

The integrity with which we pursue truth frees us to accept whatever God reveals. We do not have to echo what others think. Only as we discover that truth which satisfies our own mental integrity can we know the freedom of learning. Jesus never forced a doubtful Thomas to accept something, which violated his integrity, but rather gave him an opportunity to discover resurrection reality. With the Holy Spirit as our guide, we can study the scripture as well as life with integrity.

Let us never follow a lie simply because it is easier or more popular. We do not have to assassinate our brains nor violate our intellectual integrity to be a disciple. We are called to love the Lord with all our mind as well as our heart. The quality of our witness is based on the integrity of our knowing in Whom we have believed. Knowledge and not ignorance was our Lord's contribution to a stale spiritual environment. He along can redeem us from a religious climate that is more committed to worldly success than personal integrity.

Put On a Happy Face

Have you ever considered the ingredients of an ugly face or the makeup of a pretty one? Ugliness is not always the result of cosmetic blemishes nor is beauty the product of perfect skin. Both are reflections of inner attitudes that come from the core of our being. Some folk have a beautiful countenance even though their physical attributes are limited. Others are ugly even though they are beauty candidates. If "beauty is as beauty does" then "ugly is as ugly does." Our thoughts and our actions have far more to do with our attractiveness or lack of it than any physical qualities we may possess.

The ancient Hebrew writers used the heart as a symbol of one's inner thought processes. The Psalmist cried, "Create in me a clean heart, O God." Proverbs tell us, "As a man thinketh in his heart so is he" and "a merry heart produces a cheerful countenance." Jeremiah explains that the heart is deceitful above all things and desperately wicked. Ezekiel reminds us that God can give us a new heart and a new spirit. Jesus said, "Blessed are the pure in heart." The writer of Hebrews summarized it all when he wrote, "It is a good thing that the heart be established with grace." Scripture makes a strong case for soul beauty, which is the first step in good grooming.

However, we may look on the outside is largely determined by what we are on the inside. If one has a sour disposition it will most likely be revealed in facial expression. A negative, hateful attitude produces frowns, snarled lips and ugly contortions. One does not complain and criticize with a beautiful smile. It takes an ugly face to express our deep-seated hostility. Hate has a way of taking its toll on eyes that without it would have a peaceful gaze and on cheeks that otherwise would be flush with sweetness. Pride and greed give our faces a stern and determined look. Expressions of worry and fear create wrinkles that are unbecoming. Sorrow gives our face a sad look as despair is written boldly across our brow.

A happy heart, however, creates a pleasant countenance. Faith has a way of bringing out the smile in us. Our conversation with God adds a dimension of beauty to our facial features. The light within us cannot be hidden behind a frown. It bursts forth in the glow of a tranquil appearance. So cheer up brothers and sisters, and live in the sunshine. Let the smile of God shine through you as your face reveals the joy within. Put on a happy face because ugliness as well as beauty is somewhat contagious.

Dealing with Dislike

Do you ever wonder why it is that some people do not like you? No matter what you do or don't do, they find you rather repulsive. Since it is a normal tendency to want people to like us, we often grieve when their dislike is obvious. Our frustrations are compounded when, to us, there are no apparent reasons for their rejection. It hurts to feel the hate of others when, in our hearts, we know it is not our intention to hurt anyone. If we are people who provoke conflict, then we can expect some "eye for an eye" reactions. But if, in the sincerity of our souls, we promote peace, then it is strange when others do not respond peaceable to us.

It seems that some folk need a few people toward whom they have an adversarial relationship, and at times we become their victims. It may be that we remind them of someone who hurt them in the past. It may be that we did not have the same opinion on some issue, and some people have tender egos when it comes to disagreement. Perhaps we do not share the same enemies, and that creates problems for folk with hostile attitudes. Again, it may be that we are perceived as being different, and for some, conformity is a religion. There are a variety of ways to analyze the dynamics of people's dislike of us for no apparent reasons.

Our healthiest response, however, is not analysis but confidence. If to our own selves we have been true, we must never allow the disapproval of uncomplimentary folk to distract us from life's pursuit of happiness and purpose. Our strength can be the strength of ten if our hearts are pure. We must humbly accept the fact that everyone is not going to like us. Our task as Christians is to make sure we do not give anyone legitimate reasons for their dislike.

When there are offenses, as surely there will be, there must be the grace of apology and forgiveness. There is a sense, however, in which we must not nervously try to please everyone; else we become moral and spiritual jellyfish. We take our stands, live life to its fullest and let God be God. There is surely something to be learned from our Lord when He told His disciples to beware "when all men speak well of you."

Sin Made Easy

There is a subtle simplicity to sin, which makes it easy for us to succumb to its appeal. Most of the time we sin because it is the easy way. Seldom, if ever, do we sit down and plan a complicated agenda of disobedience. It is not the avowed intention of most of us to sin. We do so because our discipline is weak. By being carelessly indifferent to that which is high and holy, we accept that which is vain and vulgar. For the most part, we are not bad people in terms of peddling our impurities. We simply do not have the backbone to stand for the right and discourage the wrong.

We are sinners because we often follow the path of least resistance. We would rather blend into a sinful, secular culture than go to the trouble of having to explain why we are different. It is too embarrassing and time-consuming for us to put Christ first in every situation. Therefore, we go sinning along through life, not because we want to, but because it is more convenient. We reflect the popular prejudices and unfounded opinions of our day, not so much that we agree, but because it is easier to get along by going along. It requires too much mental and spiritual energy to think through situations until we have arrived at proper ethical and moral conclusions.

Sin will always give us a simple answer to complicated matters and make us feel good about our ignorance. Jesus came teaching that, "The way is hard that leads to life and few there be who find it." He understood the appeal of evil's broad road that leads to destruction and sought to warn us about our careless participation in godless chatter and behavior. Of course, it is a tough world in which to be good. Yet, the value of doing so is even more rewarding. The good life challenges the best that is within us. We must and we can survive the mediocrity of sin, but only if we are willing to yield our minds to God's truth, our hearts to God's love, and our lives to God's kind of life.

Our Story

Whether we realize it or not, each of us has a story that is of vital interest to God. It is a story of how we came to be and of the family to which we came. It is a story of the influences upon our lives, which cause us to think the way, we think and to do the things we do. It is a story about people who have impacted our lives for better or for worse. It is a story about sin and failure as well as goodness and success. It is a story with unbelievable power to control the rest of our lives. Our story is one we have to own. We cannot rewrite the script to give it a more pleasant flow, nor can we make it sound like the story others have told. It is our story, full of all the personal dreams and tragedies that compose our individual histories.

No one's story is perfect. They are all fraught with regrets and disappointments. Yet, there can be some chapters, which give us a sense of pride. We do well to accept our story as it is because the rest of our story requires a healthy understanding of what has transpired. The exciting thing about life, however, is the fact that there is a point in which our story intersects THE STORY. To say that God is interested in our story is another way of saying, "God so loved the world, that He sent His only begotten Son." God wants the loving story of His Son to be a part of our story. Although there is much about our stories that are contradictory to His story, God wants us to know that while we were yet sinners, while we were still struggling with our stories, Christ died for us.

The impetus of this truth makes it possible for us to own our stories, to confess the past and find a better way to write the future. This does not mean that our story will have no painful paragraphs. It does mean that our story will have a happy ending. God's story has redemptive possibilities for us, and we do well to make it ours. Only as His loving story becomes a part of our story will we have "a story to tell to the nations."

The reason God is interested in our story is that He makes it a part of His story. What He has done for us He can do for others, and that is the rest of the story. Will you help Him tell the good news by living the good news? It's the best way of making your story worth reading.

Grace Abuse

One of our most subtle sins is our tendency to abuse grace. How often we misuse the gracious gestures of others as well as the grace of God. It seems that we are forever taking advantage of those who would shower us with courtesy and kindness. Friendships are sometimes used to get us where we want to go. Loving people become expendable in the process. It is sad when we fail to appreciate the pain of those who must forgive us. We do well to realize how much our personal happiness depends on the fact that we are not always made to pay in full for our personal blunders.

There are folk who will deal graciously with us even though we may trample upon their feelings at times. There are people who do not live with a tit-for-tat mentality. They feel no need to properly punish everyone who has erred against them. These "grace givers" add a sense of healing worth to our lives. Their disposition of love stands in judgment on the get-even attitude so prevalent in our society.

How blessed we are to understand the vast amount of forgiveness we require and receive every day. Only God in heaven can equip us to respond graciously toward one another, and yet we consistently abuse His mercy. How often is sin minimized in our minds, simply because we know He is slow to anger and full of everlasting kindness? We sin so much it is a shame to call upon His holy name and ask forgiveness of that same sin which we repeat over and over again. In our selfishness pursuit of life's dreams, we lose sight of God's grief over our iniquities. We prefer not to meditate upon divine disappointment for fear it would interfere with our personal happiness.

The opposite, however, is true. Our inner happiness and peace of mind are strongly related to our desire to please God. In pleasing Him, we fulfill all the requirements for successful living. The grace of God always represents that which is best for us.

Whatever chastisements life may impose upon us, God has a loving purpose for our future. We never sin away our right to approach the

Secret Hideaway

There is a lonely place to which hurting people sometimes go. It is called "withdrawal." They go thinking they have found a safe haven from their woes. They wrap themselves in an emotional cocoon as a cushion against their pain. They internalize their grief and often get locked into a rut of only one way of thinking. Their imaginations play tricks on them as they lose touch with reality. Many times withdrawal causes folk to lash out at those who love them most and could care for them best. It is not easy dealing with life's complications, but retreating within oneself does not make it easier. People who turn inward to lick their own wounds have a limited source of healing.

Living with loneliness is a pain our Lord does not wish us to have. His invitation in times of despair is quite obvious. His friendship is as close to us as our ability to pray and seek His face. His word becomes our comfort, His presence becomes our strength, and His promises become our hope.

Whenever we tend to withdraw He wants to share our inner feelings. He wants to correct and caress our awkward thoughts. Because He is a man of sorrows and acquainted with grief, He understands the deepest wounds of our broken hearts. If we invite Him into the secret hideaway of our souls, He will help us keep our perspective. He will not remove the possibility of pain, but He will guide us through its adventure.

Of course, there is value in withdrawal if we understand the dynamics of our loneliness. Being alone can give us time to sort through our thoughts. It can give us a humble and contrite heart. The silence of our soul is a time for God to speak to us. On several occasions Jesus had to withdraw from the crowds in order to have time with God the Father. It was a constructive retreat from public scrutiny and the clamoring demands upon His time. He came back with renewed energy for His messianic assignments.

Our Lord is a good model of mixing our public and private needs. We must never get so public that we lose our depth of concentration. Neither should we become so private that loneliness conquers our happiness. May our symptoms of withdrawal be occasions for hearing His still small voice because He is the Lord of our inner sanctum and the salvation within our secret hideaway.

Learning to Survive

Life is not an easy journey. It is filled with much heartache and pain. The struggle to survive is one of our most demanding tasks. To survive emotionally we develop a flexible mentality. To survive spiritually we find a faith for every circumstance. To survive economically we are sustained by a proper work ethic. To survive physically we depend on proper medical principles. To survive socially we learn how to make friends and influence people. The real world in which we live offers much resistance to our survival. We are not guaranteed a free ride. We pay our dues, and sometimes we pay penalties, which are severe.

The joy of the journey, however, is in our ability to adapt. Just as life offers much resistance it also has many resources. Circumstances, which can drain us of our joy, can also strengthen us for the journey. For the most part we are created with a survival mentality. We have a capacity to find beauty in the midst of life's ugliness. We can focus on the future rather than fumble with past failures. We can confess our trespasses as we forgive those who trespass against us. We can trust God with the most delicate issues of our lives. We can search for peace in the midst of turmoil. We can find hope in the throes of despair. We can seek love in the context of hate. We can believe in life when death seems powerful. We can develop friends as we present ourselves friendly. We are created enough like God to act godly. No, life will not always treat us kindly, but we are equipped to survive.

We admire poets, artists, musicians and those who expose us to the fine arts. Yet, there is a sense in which we are all poets even though our lives do not rhyme. We are all artists even though our paintings are not professional. The melody of our experiences makes us all musicians. We are historians as we add the chapters of our lives to the accumulated history of all humankind. We cannot escape the fact that, for better or worse, we have faced the challenge of our times and in some measure we have survived. Whatever else there may be about us remains to be seen, but for now, we trust the eternal goodness of God to see us through. "He who began a good work in us will perform it until the day

Forgetfulness

Forgetfulness is a terrible curse on the human mentality. It is a condition that often increases with age and causes much embarrassment and pain. How stupid we feel at times when we have forgotten an important matter on the agenda of our lives. How hurt we are when someone forgets us in our moment of need. We wring our hands in frustration trying to adjust to the many anxieties of forgetfulness.

At the deepest level, however, adjustment to it is a spiritual matter. Forgetfulness, like all other weaknesses, must be approached from the perspective of grace. Forgiveness is the key. We must forgive ourselves, so that we can confess our forgetfulness as a part of our human frailty. To deny our tendency to forget is to open ourselves to dishonesty and irrational excuses.

We must also forgive others who equally struggle with this common ailment of humankind. It is vital to our happiness to understand that to be forgotten at some critical moment does not necessarily mean rejection. It is not an occasion for resentment and rage. After all, sooner or later, we, too, will be the forgetter. Let us treat others as we would like to be treated when we forget.

Here again, love and grace determine our peace of mind. Honesty in admitting our momentary loss of memory is much better than struggling with lame excuses. We all sin and come short in the matter of forgetting. Therefore, let us not forget to forgive forgetting.

Prayerograph

The instinct to pray is one of the basic responses of our human nature. There is something deep within us that cries for the attention of God. There is something about us, which longs to communicate with Him who is Creator and Lord. Even those with little or no spiritual ambition have moments when they want a word with Someone who is bigger than their unmanageable predicaments. A sense of helplessness and hurt often drives us to our knees in search of some healing balm. Life is too demanding and unpredictable to face without some divine conversation.

Although this inherent need to talk with God may not always find expression in a formal, disciplined prayer life, it is nonetheless a type of prayer. In fact, if cultivated, it may lead to a more personal quiet time with God. To experience God's love in the midst of our dependency and vulnerability causes us to nurture a more intimate fellowship with Him. To feel the freshness of His forgiveness encourages us to confess our sins. To sense His grief over our transgressions motivates us to forsake them. To know He cares about every aspect of our lives gives us an agenda for our daily prayers.

We are taught to pray by praying and listening. This is why Bible study and prayer go hand in hand. The Bible is a guide to keep our prayers honest. To study the prayer lives of those who really prayed shames us out of our dull, overused prayer patterns. We learn that prayer talk can be natural and conversational.

God does not require pious platitudes and meaningless catchwords. We talk to God like we normally talk. When we first learned to talk, we learned the words of prayer. There is no special vocabulary for conversation with God. Whether public or private, we simply share our thoughts with Him.

It is fellowship and not formality, which our Lord desires. He is much more interested in what we are thinking than how we articulate it. God wants to hear the sincere expressions of our own souls, not the warmed over words of someone else's prayer. It is a gesture of His grace that

Struggling Faith

Do you think sometimes we are guilty of professing a faith we do not have in order to create a faith we want? Do we talk more faith than we really believe? Are we whistling in the dark when in reality the dark has consumed us? We want to believe in that which seems impossible and we want to trust the hidden powers of God. Yet, somehow our fickle faith is plagued by doubt and we find ourselves questioning every miracle.

We are obsessed with the need to understand and to explain. We are terribly suspicious of things that look too supernatural. It is as though we are afraid God will converge upon us and then we will have to explain the things that happen to us in terms of faith. It seems at times we are actually embarrassed to acknowledge the input God has in our lives. We refuse to confess that which others might find difficult to believe.

Then, why do we talk so much about faith? Is it because deep down we know our faith is lacking and we try to encourage it by conversation? Perhaps we can find some comfort in the fact that "faith as a grain of mustard seed will remove mountains." It might just be that our simple faith can remove some mighty mountains in the hands of a mighty God. How well do you believe? As our faith matures so will our ability to trust in a God of amazing possibilities.

Painful Servanthood

Have you ever considered what kind of world this would be if every good deed were prosperously rewarded and every evil deed adequately punished? There is a subtle kind of misunderstanding about life, which assumes that righteousness is without pain and wickedness is always confounded. The truth of the matter is that sometimes good people suffer and sometimes evil people live in relative ease.

Perhaps we would prefer that God prosper the good folk and cause the evil ones to live in poverty. We want good things to happen to good people and bad things to happen to bad people. Life doesn't seem to work this way. It rains on the just as well as the unjust. Catastrophe is no respecter of persons. What then do we learn about life's inconsistent tendency to bring about pain and prosperity wherever it wishes?

For one thing, we learn that our relationship to God is one of commitment, which carries no guarantee of material benefit. Our truest love for God is a spontaneous response to who He is, rather than to what He can do for us. God continually calls us into a painful servanthood where He sooths our wounds with inner satisfaction and peace of mind.

We also learn to care for life's casualties; and if material prosperity should come our way, we effectively express our Christian stewardship. We further learn that life does not always conform to our rigid assumptions. It is always changing, and thus it requires us to adjust and to trust in God who leads us through every uncertain and unsettling situation.

We cannot always know the meaning of the moment, but we can know the Maker of it. In reality we are forced to learn that we are not ultimately in charge of our own destinies. Circumstances continue to explode the myth that we are the masters of our fate.

Of course there are magnificent reasons for us to be good and faithful

Pride

Pride is often projected as a hideous sin, which has a terrible capacity to make us appear pompous and arrogant. It creates within our egos a need to make braggadocios claims and unrealistic promises. Pride can be the root of all sin, which centers in self and personal glory. The tendency is to declare ourselves the winner in every issue. It is a pride-filled mind that assumes no one's opinion is equal to ours. It is a pride-centered heart that requires love without giving ourselves away. It is a pride-affected life style that is continually seeking the limelight. It is a pride-dominated disposition, which causes us to be rude and inconsiderate. It is a proud and haughty spirit, which our Lord cannot tolerate.

Pride, however, does not need to have such a devastating effect upon our personalities. There is a sense in which we cannot be humble unless we have that for which we can be proud. Otherwise we are just plain inferior. Pride that is tempered with love can give us the courage to witness. Pride that is born out of honest achievement can produce healthy, satisfying rewards. Pride that emerges from a submissive spirit can equip us with moral fortitude. Pride that is bathed in the tears of our own repentance can give us the strength to try again.

No, pride does not have to be the source of our sin. It can be the energy of our righteousness. It can motivate us to be the best we can be for God. It can be the inspiration of our dreams even as it contributes to the quality of our daily routine.

Perhaps the best way to deal with a damaging pride is to learn how to make it our servant rather than our master. No one can ever reach his or her full potential without some pride. Yet, no one can ever reach that potential if pride is all he or she has. It is an awesome miracle when our natural pride is transformed into spiritual ambition. Then and only then can we truly give God the glory for the great things He has done.

Disposition

Disposition is a fascinating feature of our human personality. It is that part of our inner being which shows. It defines the way we habitually react to life's situations. It is the most obvious revelation of who we are. In fact, we are known by our disposition. People will often judge us for good or bad depending on what they read from our disposition. Of course there are times when our disposition is good and there are times when it is bad. Many factors converge upon us to determine our disposition in a given situation. Most of the time, however we are fairly predictable in the way we respond to a given set of circumstances. This predictable is most likely the disposition for which we are known.

Some big questions emerge; Are we pleased with the way others see us? Does our disposition define who we really want to be? Is this window to our souls showing the best of us or the worst of us? To honestly answer these questions might be the beginning of an improved disposition.

Often, as Christians, we forget that attitude is also a part of our witness. Paul said, "Let this mind (or disposition) be in you which was also in Christ Jesus." An authentic relationship with Christ will be validated by our disposition. It doesn't ring true if we claim to have Christ in our hearts and always react like the devil.

To have a Godly disposition means that we are disposed to pray, to repent, to forgive, to love, to study, to worship and to be involved in those kinds of things which cleanse our inner being. After all, a disposition can be no better than its source of origin. We cannot expect to have the mind of Christ if the mind of the world dominates our attention. Who we really are, will often be revealed by our responses. Only God can heal a diseased disposition.

In the Beginning, God

O Lord, my God. You are a mighty being. I celebrate Your creative ingenuity. I marvel at the mystery of Your ways and the power by which You perform Your purpose. Your power is superseded only by Your grace, which produces a caring disposition in all circumstances. Your loving kindness has created a climate for my conversation with You.

You have made me with a capacity to be curious and for that reason I am filled with wonder and awe. My eager imagination causes me to reflect upon how it was in the beginning. From my limited human perspective, I imagine You busying Yourself with creations' chores. I can see You flinging stars, moon and sun into their places and putting planets into their orbits as You decorate the heavens for centuries of celestial observation.

In my mind's eye, I see You selecting planet earth as a special garden to express the beauty of Your creative skills. I observe You spinning it around the sun in such a way that its seasons offer heat and health for all kinds of living things. I see You setting in motion a variety of laws and principles, which my most scientific thoughts have yet to grasp. I imagine You calling forth all the elements of earth and arranging them in geometric continuity. I see You looking out over Your created order and You are pleased.

The beauty, which my imagination is able to behold, is limited only by my lack of vision. I stop short of seeing ultimate reality because sin and time have dulled my senses. My grasp is limited but my appreciation for that which I do not comprehend is enhanced by Your inspiration.

As I watch You moving amid that which You have made, I detect a note of loneliness. You have no one with whom to share Your marvelous universe. I wonder what is going through Your mind. And then I see You bend over and tenderly form a bit of dust into Your own image. You breathe into that lifeless form the breath of life and it becomes a living being.

A smile comes across Your face and then a sense of sadness. You have created humankind who can give You delight but may also give You grief. You are God and You are Glory. I praise You because I am wonderfully made.

But who am I that You are mindful of me? Who am I to have the benefit of Your inspired thoughts? Who am I to deserve this breath of life and this moment of grace? Who am I to think I could even imagine creation's mystery? I want to be Your humble servant who longs not only to dream about You, but to dream with You. May my thoughts before You give me a power surge for future challenges. AMEN

Scars

The scars of the past reveal two things about us. For one thing, they remind us we have been injured. Secondly, they indicate healing has happened. The important thing to note here is that we are free to focus our attention on either of these two facts. If we choose, we can allow our scars to keep our injuries ever before us. We can permit them to nag us with repeated anxiety. We can rapidly recall all those folk who have caused us pain. We can continually curse the circumstances that have hurt us. If we get angry enough, we can even shake our fist at God for allowing us to have troubled times.

Bathing ourselves in self-pity, we may find a few people who will join us in our tub of tears. Some, whose scars are fresh and wounds open, may find our whining attractive and surround us with an insidious pity party.

Yes, scars can be a terrible reminder of the bad things, which have happened to us. Yet, if we surround ourselves with folk who keep us focused on the hurt, we will never learn the lesson of our scars.

On the other hand, however, our scars can help us focus on healing rather than hurt. If we choose, we may gratefully remember the processes of healing as our wounds were repaired.

From physical injury to spiritual pain we saw forgiveness and grace at work. The scars of both instill memories of hope, as we trust God's healing power.

We may finger lovingly the pages of scripture that brought health to our souls. In love, we may rejoice over the growth that came through our painful chastisements. In faith, we may place the scars of our past into the nail-scarred hands of Jesus, as we celebrate the future. Yes, scars are signs that healing has happened. How do you see your scars?

Conviction with Courtesy

Why is it that some folk in their attempt to defend what they consider to be a Godly view of something, act so ungodly in their support of it? Why do they choose to be discourteous and crude in the affirmation of their convictions? To hear some church folk talk it sounds like they would half kill anyone who disagreed with their views. What has happened to the spirit of Jesus who taught us to be wise as serpents and harmless as doves and would not permit Simon to fight for Him?

Personal views are weak, no matter how correct they are, when they have to be defended by ugliness and a spirit of contention. Such harsh argumentation reveals not so much an interest in God's view but in promoting the pride of one's own thought. A sinful ego cannot face another point of view without a fight. Insecurity of thought will always create an argumentative attitude. Someone who is comfortable in his or her own theological skin will be courteous in the presentation of his or her convictions. There will be kindness in disagreement.

The truth of the matter is when one has a Godly viewpoint he or she will also have a Godly attitude. When one is thoroughly immersed in the truth of God he or she has nothing to prove only something to share. A Christian witness is one whose disposition verifies the accuracy of stated convictions. It will always be open, however, to other revelations as the Holy Spirit leads. Our earnest prayer, therefore, is for meekness even as He gives us courage.

The God of Our Imagination

Do we worship a god, sometimes, who is the figment of our imagination? Do we create a god in our image rather than conform to the image of God created within us? Do we set our own agenda or do we seriously search for the will of God? False gods do not have to be made out of gold or silver. They can be the products of our speculation. Idols are formed in our minds long before they are created by our hands. Our most common human heresy is to make up our own set of rules. We pray to a god who permits. We serve a god who satisfies our carnal desires. Our religion is egocentric rather than theocentric. We invent ways to satisfy our thirst for heaven, which fall short of heaven's expectations. We are never at peace with God because the gods we create instigate chaos.

Sooner or later our house of religious cards will tumble. The bubble of synthetic spirituality will burst. The charade of pretentious Christianity will end. We cannot go on serving a god who does not exist. There comes a time when the issues of life demand a quality commitment to reality. Whenever sickness and death sting us with the tentacles of despair, we need an eternal hope. Whenever temptation lurks at the door and sin creates an uneasy conscience, we need more than a silly system of self-approval. Whenever friends turn against us and we feel alone, we need the deeper friendship of divine devotion. Whenever crises come, as surely they will, we need more than human resources. Simply stated, there comes a time when we cannot make it with a faith based only on convenience.

What, then, shall we do to cultivate an authentic attachment to our Lord and all that adds substance to the living of our days? We need to take God at His word and follow His guidelines for godly living. We must evaluate our tendencies to be less than honest with ourselves about God. We cannot serve a god who exists only in our imaginations. The altar of our own ego is a poor place to find the peace that passes all understanding. We need to confront our risen Savior and in the fellowship of His suffering find meaning in whatever penalties and blessings life presents us. We are never nearer to God than when we denounce our idols and make Him the primary focus of our lives.

Our Way of Seeing Things

A fact we often fail to admit is that we do not always see things as they are, but as we are. It is the state of our own inner being, which determines our interpretation of life's happenings. This is not to say we are purposely dishonest about our views. It is a reminder that our objectivity is influenced by many outside factors. We are conditioned to believe what we believe by many circumstances over which we have had little control. We were born into a family of thought patterns and preconceived notions from which we rarely depart. Seldom do we go against the political, educational, racial and religious environment that has birthed us. We are cradled in the arms of a set of precepts we were taught would last forever.

This is not bad as long as we are willing to think for ourselves and make such truths a part of our own value system. We must distinguish, however, between inherited ideas and a personal encounter with God. So often we accept what is handed down with no questions asked. It is not until our faith is tested that we begin to scrutinize the content of our beliefs. There is emotional and spiritual strength in knowing what we believe and why we believe it. At some point along the journey we must stop living like spiritual parasites trying to imitate the faith of our fathers. Only when it becomes our faith do we fully appreciate what it meant to our fathers.

We are wise indeed if we understand the dynamics of a variety of influences that have converged upon us to make us who we are and cause us to think our kind of thoughts. Such knowledge frees us from inherited prejudices and enables us to find the truth that can make us free. Such freedom gives us a more objective way of looking at life's events. We can begin to see things more as they are rather than as we are. We are able to shed our souls of biases, which keep us chained to an unquestioned tradition.

Jesus came into the world with no preconceived notions. He was not locked into any set of principles He felt compelled to defend. He had departure from rules and regulations they held more holy than God Himself. Yet, Jesus saw things as they really were and made pronouncements on the basis of that reality.

He offers us the same spiritual objectivity today if we hunger for His truth and love. So, "let this mind be in us which was also in Christ Jesus." Who knows, we may find the courage to admit some errors of thought, as we trust God who alone sees things as they really are.

Patience

As our Christian lives develop, patience becomes the key to the caliber of our commitment. It determines the depth of our perseverance. It controls the quality of our thoughts and actions. Through patience we acquire the skills to face life's annoying circumstances. Patience creates an inner tranquility that adds smoothness to life's ruffles. It defeats fear through faith. It controls dissension with love. It conquers despair with determination. It offers hope in the midst of that which seems hopeless. Patience combines the energy of trust with the spirit of obedience to create a godly attitude and lifestyle.

At no other time are we nearer the Lord's dream for our lives than when we express patience. He calls us into the kind of life, which requires us "to wait upon the Lord." When patience is absent we often move ahead of God with devastating results. We hurry through life unwilling "to be still and know that He is God."

Our prayers quickly evaporate in selfishness and futility. We lose our quiet moments of unhindered worship. When patience is absent we lose the spiritual stamina to keep God as the focal point of our lives. Our thoughts focus on the trivial and our energy is wasted in meaningless pursuits.

Without patience we run the risk of losing control of all our virtues. In haste we say things we do not mean. In moments of anxiety we do things we later regret. In anger we hurt those we love most. In restlessness we create problems for everyone with whom we share a bit of life. In bitterness and rage we lose the ability and the desire to forgive. Without patience the vision of grace escapes us. Our nervous energy plays havoc with our health and our only hope is for patience to save us from ourselves.

The calming effect of our own personal commitment to God is no doubt the answer to our struggle for patience. In Christ Jesus we experience the ingredients for a patient mentality and the prospect for an unfaltering

Dealing with Spontaneity

In many ways we are rather spontaneous in the way we approach life. With most issues we tend to "shoot from the hip." Many of our decisions are made on the spur of the moment. Much of our conversation is the product of sentences quickly made. Careless speech flows when little thought is given to what is being said. The mismanagement of words can often lead to multiple misunderstandings.

Anger can be the result of spontaneous comments. Hasty reactions come from the lack of contemplation. Quick decisions can be devastating with long-term penalties. Since most circumstances do not allow ample time for thinking it through, how do we prepare ourselves for the spontaneity of life? How do we equip ourselves for the daily emergencies, which require words of wisdom correctly spoken? When life hands us a spur-of-the-moment situation, how do we deal with it constructively?

Of course there are no canned solutions to every predicament. There are no pat answers to every question. There is no indexed "How To" book on life's problems. There is, however, a disposition of grace with which to face the complexities of life. It is cultivated through a personal relationship with Jesus Christ. In Him we have a premeditated approach to every emergency. We call it "prayer" and "meditation" and all those moments when we reflect on the things of God.

Through fellowship with the Father we train our minds to think good thoughts, to pursue truth, to express love, and to approach each day with a constructive attitude. This does not mean we will always do and say the right thing. It does mean we will find a valuable resource in humility, forgiveness, and grace. Our obnoxious determination to prove something will not hinder our ability to learn something. From this perspective life flows with a smoother temperament.

Preparation for the spontaneity of life is a daily assignment. Just as nourishment for our bodies keeps us physically fit, so the nourishment for our souls keeps us spiritually alert. We feed on the bread of heaven and drink from the fountain of love. We allow ourselves to be washed in the blood. We bring our burdens to the Lord and leave them there.

We hide His words in our hearts that we may not sin against God. In the gradual growing of the grace and knowledge of our Lord there emerges a sweeter spirit within. Therefore, as we face the spur-of-the-moment aspects of life, "What a friend we have in Jesus."

Olympic Faith

One of the exciting things about the Christian faith is that it challenges the best that is within us. It will never let us be satisfied with inferior living. It reaches into the depths of our inner being with disturbing implications. There is no way we can look into the face of Jesus and be content with halfhearted devotion. He calls us away from everything that would make us less than what we can be. He nudges us toward everything that focuses on our spiritual potential. He inspires us to consider the high road of what is best for us rather than the low road of what is easiest for us. Like an Olympic athlete training for perfection our Lord equips us to dream His kind of dreams. No one expects as much from us and yet comforts us when we miss the mark.

The tremendous challenge of being a Christian gives life its greatest sense of purpose. Without this struggle toward some degree of excellence we would lose ourselves in the monotony of mediocrity. There is more to us than what we normally accept. We frequently underestimate our capacity for godliness. We fail to stretch our humanity because our expectations are too low. We are created to move onward and upward. To sense some progress on the journey is a great source of fulfillment. We have no better gauge of how we are doing than the gospel of our Lord Jesus. It tells us that "nobody" can be somebody and that anybody can belong to everybody in Christ Jesus. The process toward achievement keeps us believing there is a place for us in God's scheme of things.

Let us, therefore, never minimize the demands of Christianity. It is harder than any other lifestyle because it brings out the best within us. If we sentimentalize our faith and turn discipleship into a syrupy ceremony we miss the meaning of commitment and sacrifice. We must never try to camouflage the cross lest we lose the strength of its dying love. God gave His best to show us what is best for us. Indeed His greatest challenge to us is to be baptized with His baptism and to drink from His cup of pain. In the difficulty of our task we will find His glory as we faithfully pursue His dream for us.

Seasonal Perspectives

Autumn Leaves

Watching as the autumn leaves
Fall gently all around;
Their beauty once on trees displayed
Lie motionless on the ground.

Their falling, though sad, it seems
Is truly not for naught.
They form a needed cushion
For our noonday woodland walk.

So hurry on you falling leaves,
Be on your cheery way.
You seem like happy children
Dancing as you play.

You've said "goodbye" to summer sky,
"Hello" to autumn's wind.
The welcome mat of winter
is just around the bend.

Find your special hiding place
As you settle far below;
Leaving your lovely limb on high
To rest beneath the snow.

Your tree is now more stately.
The limb on which you grew
Is stronger, longer, more mature
In giving itself to you.

Goodbye for now you little leaf.
Gladly, I wait your successor
As springtime once again
Becomes nature's dressmaker.

Thanksliving

There are times when it seems that life has given us a bum rap. We turn a corner, and suddenly, a whole flurry of circumstances converge upon us with devastating effects. As we seek the meaning of life's problems, we become mired in the mud of depressing definitions. The more we talk about things, the worse they get. A ray of hope begins to emerge, however, when we no longer demand a better set of circumstances and we seek to develop a better attitude. A disposition of despair will always keep us looking on the bad side of everything. Within our own mental frame of reference to the way things are, there is the spiritual capacity to cope. We deny God's image within us when we ignore our deeper resources for hope. Of course, there are enough troubling things about life to give us valid reason to complain. Yet, our strength is not the product of fussiness but faithfulness.

Our perception of life is greatly enhanced when we can put it in its proper perspective. A young quadriplegic was asked by an insensitive social worker if he ever wished he had never been born. With a smile he responded, "I would not have missed being alive for anything. I am grateful for every moment." Isn't it strange how some folk grow resentful and look upon life as a bad bargain, while others keep singing the song of life though terminally ill?

The key to our ability to adjust to the things, which happen to us, is in our capacity to be thankful. Gratitude is something we choose. It is a decision we make. There are times when we cannot be grateful unless we choose to nurture a thankful attitude. This means that gratitude comes before we count our blessings, not afterward. It's when we choose to be grateful that we discover how many blessings we can count.

Thanksgiving is not just what we do when we get what we want. It's a way of living in which we are able to see what we never expected. Blessings to grateful people are always unexpected joys because they do not make excessive demands on life. It is in humble appreciation that we accept the attention God showers upon us. In all things, therefore, we give thanks knowing that we basically have no right to be bitter when the real challenge of life's obstacles is to make us better. After all real thanksgiving comes from thanksliving.

The Christmas Event

The Christmas event captures our attention in many ways. Its heavenly drama accents the extent of diving participation. Its earthly response gives evidence of human anticipation. There are many impressive features of that nativity night, which enable us to grasp the gospel of Christmas.

The humble setting in which it all occurred reveals the condescending nature of God. The Lord Jesus came from heaven's glory to be birthed with the crudest of maternity care. If God would stoop to a lowly stable to usher in His Son, then surely He would stoop to share with lowly sinners His love and grace. How could it be that the shepherds, noted for their simplicity and rugged life style, were the first to come? Was it not indicative of the fact that Jesus came to seek and to save the lost? The wise men came because their scholarly insight gave them a special revelation of God's activity. The simplest and the wisest as well as the poorest and the richest were all to share in this redeeming light.

The angelic choir reminds us that the coming of Christ was an event to celebrate. Because on that night "the heavens declared the glory of God," today we have a reason to sing. That first Christmas music has put a song in every believer's heart. It has been the inspiration of all our singing, which truly magnifies the gospel.

The threat of Herod was but a parable of the kind of world into which our Lord had come. It was a foreshadowing of the cross, which would eventually result in His painful, yet loving, sacrifice. The exodus from Egypt was symbolic of God's protection and care. The Herods of the world would not have the last word. Crucifixion would give rise to resurrection and in that power His word would go forth. Hallelujah what a Savior!

Celebrating Christmas

There is a subtle reaction to Christmas by people who find it distasteful to glamorize an event originally cast in obscurity and simplicity. These folk have difficulty giving lavished attention to a birth designed to accent the spiritual over the material, the humble over the extravagant and the profound over the frivolous. There is no hesitation from these persons to worship the Christ of Christmas. They prefer a less flamboyant way of finding meaning for the holiday season. Like the shepherds of old they come with a simple yearning to find the Christ of God.

On the other hand there are folk who pull out all the stops at Christmas. They spare no effort in making Christmas the most joyous occasion of the year. They give and sing and worship with greater enthusiasm than at any other time. In fact if it were not for Christmas their religious fervor would hardly be obvious. These people see in the Christ event a time to be extravagant. They feel that God has lavished His love upon them and, therefore, they must celebrate in keeping with His glorious contribution to their salvation. Their excess is not to ignore the simple Jesus, but like the wise men of old they worship with expensive gifts of gold, frankincense, and myrrh.

Whatever our own tastes may be, Christmas is here for us to honor the birth of our Lord. Perhaps somewhere between the simple shepherd's curiosity and the wise men's profound calculations we can find our way to the manger child. As we do let us celebrate in a way that gives greatest meaning for us to the words "God with us."

Lights

Lights are the most observable feature of Christmas decorations. In every neighborhood, in every store, along the streets, and in all the churches special lights are used to dress up our world for Christmas. All of these human-made lights are but a symbol pointing to the true Christmas light, which shines into all the world. Its radiance projects its glow of hope amid the turmoil of our times. That starlit heaven of long ago has given brightness to more than Bethlehem's stall. It has shone into the cracks and crevices of human depravity, giving love a chance to seek and to save.

The brilliance of Christmas is more than a physical light. It is the gleam of God's glory that penetrates the darkness of sin, ignorance, and pain. It is the glory of prophecy fulfilled, which created a sense of expectancy then but now gives redemptive value to those ancient words. It is the glory of a night of miracles, which causes us to celebrate like those who were closest to it. It is the glory of a virgin birth, which is the best way to describe God's participation in the event. It is the glory of life, which has come to conquer death. It is the glory of truth which has come to triumph over wrong. It is the glory of God's suffering love, which has come to break the power of human pride. It is the glory of Jesus Christ who is the true Light of the world.

So here we are once again at Christmastime trying to grasp the significance of this momentous occasion. Suddenly in the midst of all our festivities we are captured by the fact that "Christ was born of Mary this lovely Christmas day." We are overwhelmed by the sense of divine concern. We are humbled by the smallness of our own love and our own gifts. We are challenged by His grace as we see ourselves mightily in His debt. With that simple manger love of long ago we are caught up in the spirit of Christmas. It is indeed a light, which the darkness does not comprehend.

Presence in Our Presents

Two words, which sound the same but are spelled differently, have much to do with how we do Christmas. The words are "presents" and "presence." Both describe an important aspect of Christmas time. Perhaps the most popular feature of Christmas is the exchanging of "presents." In fact, it may be the pivotal point of most people's Christmas celebration. Giving "presents" at Christmas is a tradition with a long history. No one knows for sure when the practice first became a major item on the Christmas agenda.

More than likely, the idea was inspired by the Bible's reference to Jesus' birth as God's gift. Perhaps the Wise Men's appearance at the nativity event with their gifts of gold, frankincense and myrrh has enhanced the concept. Whatever its background, the giving of "presents" has captured our culture and dominated Christmas for a long time. Although it has a tendency to get out of hand, it's not an unwholesome custom. There can be a lot of affirmation and love expressed in our "presents,"

Whatever meaning our tangible "presents" may have, however, depends on how much of our "presence" is in them. How well do we give ourselves in the exchange of "presents?" When the Wise Men came with their royal "presents" the scripture, tells us they bowed down and worshiped the Christ child. Their "presents" were merely symbols of their "presence" which they brought to Jesus. Their real offering was themselves.

Here then is the proper mode of our Christmas giving. How much of our "presence" do we share with our "presents?" No matter how big the "present," it has little real worth apart from a personal investment. We love people best with our "presence" and not just our "presents." One of the benefits of Christmas is to be with those we love. The question emerges: Are we with them or just around them? To share our "presence" is to truly give ourselves to those with whom we share life. It means to give a bit of ourselves away to those who hurt, who suffer misfortune or any who need the ministry of our "presence."

God could have remained God and blessed us only with material necessities. Rather, He chose to bless us with His "presence." Therefore,

Jesus was born to be "God with us." With this in mind, we may get a new perspective on Christmas in which our "presents" and our "presence" find their proper meaning. Have a beautiful Christ-centered Christmas.

Receivers and Givers

For some folk it is more difficult to receive than it is to give. For them receiving is degrading.

It creates a situation in which they are not in control. It implies a sense of dependency upon another. Their egos are affected by the fact that someone else has the power to meet their needs.

While giving accents the prosperity and prominence of the giver, receiving requires the humble acceptance of another's good fortune.

Even when need is not the motive of giving, for some it still suggests a sense of poverty. Some people simply are not equipped to receive anything from anyone without making adequate compensation. This ought not to be.

Life at its best is a healthy combination of both giving and receiving.

Of course no one wants to be a deadbeat, yet there is a place for us to receive humbly that which others give in love.

To deny their gift is to reject their kindness. Therefore, let us graciously receive from those who wish to give and in so doing learn the lesson of grace.

The gospel reminds us over and over again that our relationship to God is that of recipient. The call of salvation is that we humbly accept His offer of love in Christ Jesus. Before grace can ever be appropriated in our live, our mood must be one of dependency and trust.

In that sense, we must first be receivers before we can ever be givers. When we understand that all we have has been received from God and others, then giving and receiving take on a new meaning. Let the gift of grace bless both your giving and receiving this Christmas.

After Christmas Letdown

When the Christmas activity is over, what then? When the carols have faded away, the gift-wrapping paper has been burned, and families have returned, what then? When the star of Bethlehem has faded into the starless heavens of human activity, what then? Is there a letdown in your life when the most exciting season of the year has ended? Do you search diligently for something to replace the emotional high of Christmas festivities? Yes, it happens to all of us to some degree, but it should not be that way.

Depression after Christmas may indicate that we missed the real meaning of His birth. Christmas is not an end. It is a beginning. It is not the only joyous time of the year, but a symbol of the joy we may have every day in Christ. To be sad after Christmas may be a natural response to the absence of loved ones and family activities. However, there can be a lingering joy of memories and meaningful times of worship.

From a spiritual perspective Christmas should be a revival of our zest for living. It should renew our capacity to trust God and one another for a happiness that is not seasonal. It should revitalize our perception of the gift of forgiveness, love and grace, which is really what that manger birth was all about.

To be sad after Christmas is to forget that God was in Christ reconciling the world unto Himself. The New Year comes to remind us that old things have passed away and that in Christ we find a place to begin again. Every day is brighter because of that Christmas star. Every song is sweeter because the angels sang. Here is where a merry Christmas gives rise to a happy New Year. May it be so for you.

A Prayer for Year's End

Lord, we come to the end of another year keenly aware that you have been involved in the particulars of our lives. We have faced a world of difficulties, heartaches and pains, but you have encouraged us to survive. You have given us occasions of joy, worship and sweet surprises to motivate us through the struggles of our daily routine. Your Holy Spirit has been the silent Partner of our lives as the energy of your love has made our living together an experience of grace.

Lord, it has not been easy to lose our loved ones, hear threats of unemployment, accept misunderstanding and face a bundle of fears. Our faith was hesitant as we waded through the accumulation of events called 2009. Yet, in retrospect, we are able to see that no single happening was able to separate us from the love of God in Christ Jesus our Lord.

We must confess, however, the error of our ways. We hang our heads in shame when we contrast your blessings and our behavior during the past year. You have been far better to us than we have been to you and to one another. Help us as we try to repent, and may we never sin away our ability to hope for a holy new year.

Thank you, Lord, for the pain as well as the joy that has contributed to the character of our fellowship with friends and loved ones. We do not know what the future holds, but we are holding on to the One who holds the future. Your blessed Son has given us renewed reason to trust one another as we trust you.

We do not necessarily pray for an easy year, but we do petition you for power to persevere. We ask for your wisdom to face the complexities of our modern world. We seek the light of your guidance down the dark path of the unknown. We knock on the door of opportunity to be your servant people. May you, O Lord, find pleasure this New Year from the words of our mouths, the meditation of our hearts and the performance of our lives.

Happy Endings

Everyone loves a story with a happy ending. We like our heroes to go riding off into the sunset to live happily ever after. We like happy endings because we want everything to turn our good in the end for ourselves as well as for people we like. Life, however, does not always give us happy endings. Some things in the story of our lives end up in disarray. There are chapters in the sequences of events that shape our lives, which have sad conclusions. Of course life as we try to put it together will have an assortment of endings. When we try to write the pages of our personal history all by ourselves, we face a barrage of unpredictable conclusions.

Only in Christ can we fully know the meaning of happy endings. Only He who is the author and finisher of our faith can write the script for our lives with positive benedictions. In Him the sins, which produce sadness, are conquered by His chastising grace. In Him the fear that produces failure is absorbed in the courage of commitment. In Him the prospects for bitterness and resentment are relieved amid His encouragement to forgive. In Christ Jesus the sad-ending chapters of our lives can enhance the beauty of our being because He works for our good in everything if we love Him and are called according to His purpose.

The fact that we shall live again in God's eternal glory means that life's episodes with unhappy endings need not lead us to despair. Our ultimate happiness is not attached to the perishable treasures of this life, but to the power and the glory of the Lord forever and ever. In Him we need never have an unhappy ending, which does not remind us that one day in Christ we shall live happily ever after.

Therefore, have a happy ending to the old year and anticipate the wonderful possibilities of the New Year. By faith the future can be brighter than the past and the present can be full of exciting expectations.

The New Year

The New Year converges upon us with the powerful impact of time. The old year has squeezed through the cracks of many passing events we thought would last forever. Days gone by rapidly fold into the pages of the past, while the days ahead are pages clean for the writing. Time is always in forward motion. Although we would like to go back and re-live some moments and re-do some deeds, we cannot. We are left with a set of memories, which serves us with a combination of both satisfaction and sorrow. Perhaps our most wholesome understanding of the present is that we are in the process of making more memories. Whatever we do today greatly affects our perspective on things tomorrow. The opinion we will have of ourselves and others tomorrow is affected largely by what happens today.

We cannot always control the things that happen to us. Life is not nearly as predictable as we often assume. We make our plans, we set our course and then the strong winds of circumstance steer us in many directions. Adjustments have to be made. Dreams have to be re-dreamed. It takes a lot of flexibility in dealing with Father Time. Only those who understand and accept the dynamics of change can be happy. Those who carve out their ruts of despair and get locked into only one of life's many channels will never know peace. Some will never sing because they have not allowed themselves to find life's melody. We cannot wait until life is entirely to our liking before we express our music. People, who lose their zest for life by whining and complaining about the passing of time, are to be pitied.

God calls us forward in faith to face a future that will yield its problems and its solutions, its sorrow and its joy, its pain and its peace, its hate and its love, its sin and its forgiveness as well as a healthy combination of fear and courage. We must be still and know that He is God, lest our urge to go everywhere and do everything affects our ability to worship and pray. In our hurry to get on with life, we may rob it of its most tender moments and its sacred purpose. We cannot stop the coming of the New Year, but we can stop fretting about the past. We can allow the Lord of all life to be the Lord of our lives and the Lord of the New Year.

Ambition

Ambition is a strange and sometimes fickle aspect of the human personality. It is a potent force, which has far reaching implications for every area of life. It is the motivational mechanism of our beings and the energy of our personalities. Rightly regarded ambition can lead us to the land of our dreams. We can climb the mountains of achievement and look out over the valleys of conquest. In the drama of our quest for success, ambition plays a leading role. It keeps us committed to whatever discipline that is required to be successful.

Godly ambition can keep us moving toward righteousness and the desire to fulfill our spiritual goals and gifts. It can keep us pressing toward the high calling of God, which we have in Christ Jesus. God has given us ambition so that we may strive to be more than mediocre. He has equipped us with a capacity to do our best. In this light, ambition is a gift from God.

On the other hand, however, undisciplined ambition can be a terrible curse. It can become an emotional prison where we are chained to the wheels of some kind of progress. Tangible achievement becomes our "god" as we risk losing our very souls in the success syndrome. Uncontrollable ambition punishes us with compulsive energies fed by the fires of obsession and fanaticism. Awkward appetites lead us toward greed and a covetous lifestyle. We are forever bound by what others think and say. The competitive spirit keeps us working harder and harder to prove our worth. We are intimidated by those who are ahead of us as well as those who are gaining on us. What a hectic way to live.

While it is healthy to have ambition and a wholesome respect for progress, it is demoralizing to have ulterior motives for success. Only in Christ can our ambition be redeemed and our spiritual goals reborn. In Him we have reached the "top" when, at the foot of the cross, we learn the real meaning of achievement and progress. No amount of religious rationalizing can make God the author of ill-gotten gain and manipulated prosperity.

Life

Life is a strange and awesome energy. Its power defies our imagination. The seed, which springs forth from the ground into a living plant, is one of nature's marvelous miracles. Plants, which lie dormant in the winter, bud in the spring, produce fruit in the summer and yield their harvest in fall, are a reminder of life's cycle of power. How strange that life emerges from an assortment of eggs, wombs and seeds. Yet volumes have been written by those who have studied the amazing realities of origins and species. Life from its simplest to its most complex forms points to a power beyond itself.

One of our most obvious truths is that life is not an invention of human ingenuity. We merely cooperate with the process. We observe its intricate mysteries. Our major contribution is to protect, appreciate and celebrate life with its many possibilities. In multiple ways all life is interwoven into a oneness. It is a oneness of survival and purpose. All living things have an innate capacity to endure. There is a reason for every plant and animal. Nothing escapes the attention of our Creator God in terms of His intentional will for everything He has created.

Because human life is spiritual as well as physical, inner growth is possible. Within the human psyche there are Godly needs, which require divine cultivation. We long for the Creator God to create and recreate within us new dreams, hopes and aspirations for all that we are capable of becoming. At best we are unfinished creatures longing for that which makes us complete. We are challenged by the unknown, stimulated by the mysterious and fulfilled by learning. There is a part of us, which surpasses our animal instincts and finds satisfaction in communion with God.

Of course there is always tension between the human and the divine. We are never as good as we hope to be and for that reason we pray and worship. We reach out to Him who is the energy of all life to equip us for the living of our days. Just as there are seasons within the cycle of nature there are seasons of the soul within the cycle of spiritual growth. Our most pertinent prayer is for the winds of God's spirit to blow away the deadness of winter's carnality and allow the blossoms of new life to usher in a springtime for our souls. So might it be in this season of hope and possibility.

The Death of Jesus

The death of Jesus carried with it the terrible stigma of crucifixion. According to the customs of His time, it was not an honorable way to die. Crucifixions were meant for murderers, thieves, insurrectionists and rabble-rousers of the worst kind. Decent folk did not participate in the horror of such executions. It was left for the cruelest of the cruel and toughest of the tough to carry out this phase of Roman justice. The reputation of crucifixion was such that it always discredited its victim. Only the most notorious criminals received such treatment.

Is it not ironic that the best God had to offer was terminated by the worst man could do? It is senseless to think that the most gentle and loving person on earth was exposed to that escalation of hate. It boggles the imagination to think that God could withhold His wrath during the torturous death of His Son. On the other hand, was it not just like Jesus to end up some place where His grace was most needful? He died just like He lived among the kind of people who were the most likely candidates for religious renewal.

He came to seek and to save the lost, and He found them in every circumstance of His life. From a jealous Herod at His birth to a conniving Sanhedrin at His death, Jesus encountered a sinful humanity. His famous prayer "Father forgive them for they know not what they do" is a summary statement of how He lived. His attitude toward sin and sinners combined condemnation and grace as the basis of holy living. "He who knew no sin became sin that we might know the righteousness of God the Father." How then can we escape if we neglect His great salvation?

The Resurrection

The spiritual and emotional energy for Christianity comes from the Resurrection. No other event is as pivotal to the expression of our faith. It is the focus of our theology. We may disagree on the particulars of our faith, but we cling to the Resurrection. Our day of worship coincides with Resurrection day. For most Christians the Sabbath gives way to Sunday simply because Jesus rose from the dead on the first day of the week. Some of our most optimistic and powerful hymns feature the Resurrection. Gospel sermons resonate with a strong emphasis on the risen Christ. It is an inescapable fact that Christians are an Easter people. We are nurtured in the Resurrection conversation.

Because of the Resurrection we are not worshipping a dead hero, but a risen Savior. Our Lord's teaching and example were good in and of themselves, but the Resurrection gave impetus to all He said and did. It validated who He was and gave credence to His proclamation. His whole life pointed to this ultimate miracle. Without it His followers could have been disillusioned by seeming defeat. Without it Christianity might not have survived the first century and the memories of those closest to Jesus.

There is a tremendous note of victory produced by the Resurrection. From the despair of Good Friday the disciples rejoiced in the presence of the risen Christ. Because Jesus survived death, hell and the grave they began to feel it was also possible for them. Because of the Resurrection there is the feeling of eternity about our life in Christ. The future loses some of its mystery because death cannot keep it prey. We began to sense that life is headed somewhere. We are not on a dead-end street identified by a grave marker. We too anticipate a resurrection.

The Resurrection is a strong reminder that evil will not have the last word. Although it seems to prevail in this life, we are moving toward its defeat. People who hate and murder, lie and steal, or cause confusion and discord are not an Easter people because Easter people rejoice in good and not evil. No one deserves it, but everyone is invited to God's great Easter party. Come, let us celebrate. He has risen. Indeed He has risen.

Resurrection Thoughts

One of the fascinating features of the resurrection is that Jesus appeared only to His faithful followers. He revealed Himself only to those who were capable of believing in the resurrecting power of love. Those who knew Him best were prepared to accept the phenomenal fact that He arose from the dead. Resurrection was not the splashy display of heavenly fireworks but the quiet celebration of humble folk whose spiritual hopes and dreams had also been resurrected. Jesus did not allow His resurrection to become a weapon against those who had created its necessity.

Had we been in charge of the resurrection, we would have given it much publicity. We would have made certain that those responsible for His death would know that their evil deed had been for naught. We would have hounded Herod, Pilate and their cohorts until we got revenge for their acts of cruelty. Most likely we would have had a rally to raise money for all who had forsaken houses and land to follow Jesus.

This is where we are so unlike our Lord. He never sought to retaliate. Never once did He intimidate or embarrass anyone into being a disciple. It was not skilled argumentation but suffering love that made Jesus our Savior. Easter was not intended to browbeat skeptics into submission but to empower saints to be instruments of His grace. The logic of love does not seek revenge; it turns the other cheek. It goes the second mile, and forgives seventy times seven.

The resurrection was never designed to display God's magic but to reveal the power of love to overcome all that hate and evil might conspire against us. Jesus did not need the resurrection to prove He was right. He used it to give us the assurance that "Lo, He is with us, even to the end of the world."

The Resurrection Event

The resurrection of Jesus is Christianity's most awesome event. It is the focal point of all our theology. It is the source of genuine excitement. It is the motivation for our preaching and the inspiration of our singing. No event in the history of humankind has offered such redemptive possibilities as the resurrection. None of the other religions of the world give us this exceptional glimpse of God.

The real power and glory of the resurrection, however, is that it transcends that first Easter morning. It is more than a historical event, it is a continuing experience. The energy of God's new life was not exhausted on His Son. His resurrection capabilities are still operative. The profound truth of Easter reminds us that God is a "dead-raiser." Not only does this have eternal implication, it has value for us in the here and now. To be dead in our trespasses and our sins is a death from which our Lord wishes to raise us. To be dead in spiritual apathy with no evangelistic zeal is a death our Lord wishes to help us conquer. To be dead in bitterness, hostility and revenge is a death our Lord wants us to survive by instilling His forgiving love. To be dead in religious hypocrisy and self-righteous superiority is a death we can overcome as our Lord teaches us the meaning of humble submission.

The spirit and power of resurrection permeate our world today, even as we celebrate The Resurrection event. The most exciting news which emerges from Easter and all of God's Word is that we do not have to stay the way we are. There is no longer a need to quarrel over who is the greatest in the kingdom of God. We serve a loving God who inspires us to seek peace. The central theme of resurrection hope is grace and not retaliation. Sin can be forgiven. Wars and rumors of war can cease. Death does not have the final word. The grave does not control our destiny. Truth marches on in spite of our puny defense. In faith, we shall overcome because, "He is not here, He is risen from the dead."

Thomas (An Easter Monologue)

"I cannot believe it! It's too preposterous! You are asking me to believe something that violates my better judgment." This was the reaction of a doubtful Thomas as the other disciples joyfully reported their encounters with the risen Lord. "You are surely mistaken," he insisted. "After all, I saw Him on the cross. I saw those horrible spikes driven through His flesh and I noted His punctured side. I saw His life's blood drain from His mortal wounds.

No! No! He was dead when they laid Him in that tomb. If He were not, He surely suffocated after being in that stale enclosure for three days wrapped in the airtight clothing of the dead. There is no way He could have survived that ordeal. When the Romans carry out a crucifixion there is no margin of error. Their executions are frightfully final.

I'll have to see for myself before I believe. In fact, I would have to see His pierced side and His nail-scarred hands. Resurrection is much too big an event for me to take someone else's word for it. I cannot say I believe when I do not. I cannot live off someone else's dream. I know you men mean well but I live in a real world. I can't trust rumor. I have to see for myself.

The truth of the matter is we had better be looking out for ourselves. The authorities will no doubt come after us next. We cannot stay hidden in this upper room forever. We must get on with our lives and do the best we can with what our Lord taught us during His short life.

Wait! Who is this? How did you get in here? Why are you holding out your hands? I see the scars and behind your robe is the pierced side. You are! You are! My Lord and my God! It's true you have indeed risen from the dead. You are the Son of God. Now I understand what you meant when you talked about dying and being raised on the third day.

resurrection possibilities. Only a few days ago you were a good teacher and friend, but now you are the risen Lord.

That news is too good to keep! I must go now and share it with others. Hey, you, did you know Jesus is risen? Yes, I know it sounds unbelievable, but I saw Him. He is alive! Come see for yourselves!"

No Cross, No Crown
(Soliloquy)

His words were clear and convincing as He said to me, "Take up your cross daily and follow me." I had wanted words of pity and comfort. I felt I had done a good job keeping His commandments and following His teachings. Could He not recognize the sincerity of my efforts? I thought I needed reassurance and perhaps a pat on the back, but the words kept coming again and again, "Take up your cross. Take up your cross."

In anguish I cried, "But, Lord, a cross is so crude and cold. It represents nothing but pain and misery. What could I possibly do with a cross?" "You could follow me," He said, as His eyes were fixed on that hill far away and a cross so rugged and despised. You could follow me unto death and receive a crown of righteousness."

"Follow You? I can't do that. I'm no Savior! I can't die for the sins of the world," I pled. "You've got me all wrong, Lord. You have mistaken me for a martyr. All I wanted was salvation, you know, a home in heaven. I just yearned for peace and quiet amid the perplexity of my daily routine. I did not volunteer to be some kind of spiritual hero." His eyes grew sad as He repeated, "Take up your cross."

"I beg you, Lord, let me be excused", I insisted. "I'm not disciple material. I cannot talk religion, and theology is too far above me. I'm just a simple-minded person who is trying to get through life the best I can. I am much too sensitive to be criticized and hurt by uncaring people. I could never minister to people who would not appreciate my efforts. No, Lord, I have no stomach for this cross business. Let me be excused."

The expression on His face changed and his mood became somber as He turned from me. The words He chose were dripping with sadness as He said, "NO CROSS, NO CROWN."

Bread and Cup

The bread and the cup of Holy Communion are simple symbols of God's enormous investment in each of us. We do not eat this bread lightly nor drink this cup carelessly lest we eat and drink damnation upon ourselves. It is not that God is going to get us if we do not do it right. It is a matter of ignoring the impetus of this communion meal. It is a matter of refusing fellowship with God, to whom the bread and the cup point. The whole of our Christian commitment focuses upon this simple gesture. The Lord God of this universe has given His Son and there are serious consequences if we reject Him. Therefore, if we are old enough and know enough and care enough, the table is a part of our covenant with God. The promises we make to God begin with the promise He has made to us by giving us this meal. We have been promised to eat anew with Him in His kingdom and we do well to eat with Him now.

When Jesus said, "This do in remembrance of me," He was making the Lord's Supper a memorial meal. It was to be a continuing reminder of God's involvement in our salvation. We eat and drink with Him lest we forget His virgin birth, His kingdom truths, His miracles of compassion, His dying love, His resurrection power, and His amazing grace. Lest we forget the cross with its redemptive implications, we re-enact that tearing of flesh and shedding of blood. Lest we forget that it was God's only begotten Son who bore that pain, we surround the table with holy reverence. Lest we forget our calling to be brothers and sisters in Christ; we pass the plate and the cup to one another in love. Lest we forget the sacrificial demands of our own discipleship, we listen as the table reminds us to "deny ourselves, take up our cross and follow Him."

There is a sense in which the Lord Himself has prepared a table before us and to eat and drink with Him is to accept His lordship and His leadership. It is an occasion to review our lives and to renew our vows. The passing of a plate of bread and a tray of cups may seem routine and outdated. Yet, the meaning of this memorial meal is more than a procedure or a ceremony. It is the picture of love in which our spiritual lives are nurtured and sustained. Come let us eat and drink together as we share in His kingdom on earth as it is in heaven.

God in the Ordinary

How strange it is that we often look for God in the bizarre and the unusual rather than seeing Him in the natural and the normal. We tend to enclose God in some deep, dark, unknowable mystery, when in reality He wishes to make Himself known in that which we can understand. We spend so much time exploring God's domain, we fail to find Him in our domain. In reality, God is as much a part of our daily routine as He is a part of those phenomenal moments that defy human explanation. Sometimes it seems we have more of an incurable curiosity for the abnormal than a sensible commitment to a daily walk with God.

It seems that we would rather be mystified than sanctified. Because we want religion to be a magical fairyland, we miss God's miraculous involvement in the normal flow of daily activities. Of course, He is Lord of the spectacular, but He is also the One who has engineered life's obvious routines. We must never allow our faith to become dependent on strange manifestations. We must not allow ourselves to become addicted to the bizarre.

Life is not lived entirely on the mountain top of emotional excitement. There is the valley of common, everyday experiences. We must find God here, also, or we will be forever wanting God to prove Himself in some sensational manner. A faith that is built primarily on dramatic episodes of unusual happenings is not faith. God is not proved by the sleight of hand. In fact, God is not proved at all. He is experienced.

Our faith is formed in fellowship with the Father. We love Him and follow Him because He is our loving Father, not because He entertains us with feats of magic. Two thieves shared Calvary with our Savior. One of them wanted Jesus to prove His power by coming down from the cross. The other thief saw His power without such proof and requested a place in our Lord's kingdom. To this man of simple faith Jesus replied, "Today you shall be with me in paradise." And so it is with all who trust God to be God.

Success and Failure

Someone has said, "Success knows no strangers while failure has no friends." On first reading it seems to be a fairly accurate observation. We do tend to applaud those who succeed and shun those who have failed. Society gives the limelight to those who have done extraordinarily well, yet it hardly gives a footnote to those who have not met public expectations. The friendship factor favors the successful. We clamor for companionship from those who can teach us how to be winners. We are indifferent to those who have allowed life to lose its zest. Business, politics, entertainment, and sometimes even religion focus upon beautiful people who appear to be bright and successful. Therefore our beginning statement seems to have some validity.

On the other hand, however, the issue of success and failure may be as much a matter of perception as reality. If we perceive ourselves to be successful, most likely we will have a more exuberant personality. Yet, if we perceive ourselves to be failures most likely we will be inhibited and withdrawn. From this perspective neither success nor failure is as much a matter of numbers as it is a matter of attitude. Successful people who have lost the challenge of achievement feel like failures. People who have failed are sometimes motivated to survive their setbacks and focus their sights on higher goals. In many ways we are who we think we are and we do well not to think more highly or lowly of ourselves than we ought.

The scripture's definition of success and failure does not conform to the world's dictionary. From the world's viewpoint Jesus did not look successful as He hung on the cross. At one point He may have felt failure and forsaken by God. Yet, as He moved through those moments of horror and put it all in God's perspective, He punctuated His achievement with the words, "It is finished." His assignment was over. He had participated in Life's most successful event.

The apostle Paul did not feel he had arrived at any great level of distinction, but he pressed on to the goal and the prize of his high calling in Christ Jesus. He had a success mentality that encouraged him to do all things through Christ who strengthened him. He would not allow himself to be defeated by harassment, persecution, or pain.

Here we sense that real success is a matter of commitment while failure is a lack of it. Perhaps we can construct a new saying, "Success is a stranger to those who allow failure to defeat them." Where are you on the scale of productive living?

The Unity of God

Sometimes in our discussion of the Trinity we talk about going through Jesus to get to God. In doing so our thoughts focus upon the fact that Jesus is our great High Priest. As the ultimate sacrifice for our sins we need no other ceremony performed by no other person to save us from the wrath of God. When Jesus died on the cross it was as if He bore all the sins of the world in His broken body. From the human perspective this vicarious death is hard to understand. Why would the God of all creation go to such extremes for His rebellious creatures? It is mind bobbling to consider the ramifications of such a deed.

He who died for our sins is also our great intercessor. The Bible pictures Jesus as being at the right hand of the Father to make intercession for us. As we pray in Jesus' name we are aware of the Holy Spirit's assistance because God has made it possible through His Son. Thus, we tend to think in terms of getting to God through Jesus.

Another way of thinking about this matter, however, is that when we get to Jesus we have already gotten to God. If we understand the oneness of the Trinity we do not have three separate Gods, but one God in three expressions. Father, Son and Holy Spirit are three ways of approaching and understanding God. Either of these is as much God as the other. Although God does not require us to have perfect understanding, we do well to sense the "Godness" that is around us, within us, and above us at all times.

The unity of God gives stability to our thoughts about divine matters. If we perceive three separate Gods then our human tendency is to accent one over the other. Theological problems arise with a "Jesus only" movement because it tends to minimize the creator God of might and glory. Over exaggeration of the Holy Spirit reduces religion to an emotional appeal where feelings supersede thinking. To focus upon "God only" as ultimate reality stretches our thought processes, but it ignores the saving love of Jesus and the abiding presence of the Holy Spirit. Perhaps Father, Son, and Holy Spirit is God's way of teaching us who He is and what He is about in His world. Hopefully, our love for God embraces every aspect of His deity. The God and Father of our Lord Jesus Christ hovers over us, teaching us through His Holy Spirit that Jesus died and rose again for our everlasting life. There is unity in the "Godness" of who we worship and we praise Him for it.

Ode to a Mother

My mother was more than a mother you see,
She was a friend as a friend was meant to be,
My mother had class and charm for her years,
As God guided her ways and soothed her tears.

It will never be easy to understand such grace
That gave me a mother whose tender embrace;
Would comfort my sorrow and ease my pain
With never a thought for her earthly gain.

I came here to be in the image of God,
My mother made sure and spared not the rod.
It's hard being reared by the Book they say;
If the Word does not quicken and change thy way.

But change there must be when a mother's prayer
Moves softly through the evening air,
And hovers the place of her children's rest,
So that God in heaven may perform His quest.

It's hard to imagine what life would have been
Without such a mother on whose love to depend.
I care not what measure it takes to express
To give God the glory for her gentle caress.

So, thank you, dear Lord, for this humble way
Of saying some things on her special day.
These words may be mine and mine alone,
Yet, to all they belong whose mother is gone.

Calvin S. Metcalf 1989

Fatherhood

The fatherhood of God is a dominant theme in the scriptures. We find a strong emphasis on it in the teachings and practices of Jesus. On several occasions He taught His disciple to think of God in terms of father. Jesus addressed His prayers to the heavenly Father and left this model for our praying as well. The earliest recorded words of Jesus, as a lad left behind in the temple, have Him referring to His "Father's business." Some of His last words on the cross were "Father into Thy hands I commend my spirit." The Father-Son relationship was highlighted throughout the ministry of Jesus. We cannot understand Jesus without grasping something of the overwhelming love of the Father and the complete obedience of the Son. Indeed, we declare they are one.

Because the word "father" has different connotations for each of us, we must see God as the ultimate, or ideal, Father. There is no way to compare "heavenly Father" with "earthly father." Human fathers are fragile and sinful. God the Father is perfect and holy. If we allow our concept of "earthly father" to determine our concept of "heavenly Father" we may have a limited perception of God the Father. It is God who gives the directions and offers the true meaning of "father." We have our heavenly Father to thank for whatever blessings we derive from our earthly father. Whatever is lacking in our earthly father's affection can be absorbed in the overwhelming love of God the Father.

With faith as our strongest ally, we reach out to God like little children who find strength and security in their father's grasp. In the family setting where a father offers kind and gentle leadership, a child is able to sense the greater love of God. It is from our fathers that we learn to appreciate the masculine side of life. If, for some reason, the family is lacking a full-time father, it is important for children to have some Christian male role models. Every child needs some significant masculine influence. When it is lacking, personality development is hindered. All men are not biological fathers, but all men can reflect the fatherhood of God. "Rise up, O men of God" and serve God in a manly

Patriotism

The spiritual implications of patriotism are as pertinent to life, liberty and happiness as any freedom, which we enjoy. In fact, there can be no real patriotism unless there is a Godly influence in our lives. At its best patriotism means that we have a caring disposition for the people with whom we share this bit of land. It involves a willingness to surrender our selfish inclinations for the good of our fellow citizens. Patriotism means that we no longer see others as stepping-stones to our own success. In other words, we put the nation above everything but God.

Of course whatever inspiration we have toward genuine patriotism comes from God. He is the One who originally initiated the governmental processes. In His wisdom He has ordained that we have laws and leaders to maintain order and to control chaos. Our Lord's strongest encouragement toward patriotism was His words "Render unto Caesar the things that are Caesar's." We cannot escape the spiritual implications of our patriotic commitment. We are called of God to add a dimension of hope and stability to our country.

The Bible and all it teaches us about living together in love and self-denial is the textbook for citizenship. Our pledge of allegiance is not only to a land but to the Lord of all creation. Our motto is a simple truth for "in God we trust" and "in God we are trustworthy." Our prayer for our country is in essence a prayer for ourselves that we be decent and caring in every aspect of our lives.

We cannot divorce who we are from what our nation is becoming. We are either part of the problem or part of the solution to the great issues, which face a country like ours. God help us to be a kind and gentle people who will not hurt others as we seek to realize our dreams. Patriotism requires that our dreams benefit "the least of these" so that there is a divine dimension to our citizenship. "God bless America" is not a song we sing only on "flag waving" days, but a prayer on the lips of all who invite God's participation in our nation's mission.

Love Will Prevail

How does love prove its power so that hate does not appear to have the advantage? How does that which is self-giving get the attention it deserves? How does unassuming humility take precedence over pride's publicity? How does the good news of grace become as attractive as the bad news of disgrace? While these are questions, which appeal to our human curiosity, they do not reflect our deepest understanding of these topics.

Love does not need to prove its power. It is power. It is the energy of sheer goodness. Love, that is out to prove something will quickly turn to hate if its point is ignored. Self-giving does not need attention. It loses itself in the cause for which sacrifices are made. It works behind the scenes so as not to distract from the issues, which are uppermost on love's agenda. Humility never seeks the headlines. It does not even advertise its lowliness lest the power of pride invade a contrite heart. Humility is a vulnerable virtue. No one can truly be humble without some reason to be proud, otherwise he or she is simply inferior.

The good news of grace never uses the methods of the world to project its message. It is attractive only to those who have eyes to see and ears to hear. Grace receives its appeal by the power of the Holy Spirit and not the energy of manipulation. The gospel is never in competition with the newsstand. Grace is always a superior word from God and does not need sensational headlines nor tricky advertisement.

What then do we say? It is love, self-giving, humility and grace that will survive and he or she who loses their life in them will find the abundant life. Whatever power or circumstance, which negatively confronts us, will have to deal with the God-given, positive, prevailing implications of love.

Bringing Out the Best

One of the exciting things about the Christian life is that it challenges the best that is within us. It will never let us be satisfied with inferior living. It reaches into the depths of our inner being with disturbing implications. There is no way we can look into the face of Jesus and be content with halfhearted devotion. He calls us away from everything that would make us less than what we can be. He nudges us toward everything that focuses on our spiritual potential. He inspires us to consider the high road of what is best for us rather than the low road of what is easiest for us. He equips us to dream His kind of dreams and offers to be with us as we pursue them. No one expects as much from us and yet comforts us when we miss the mark.

The tremendous challenge of being a Christian gives life its greatest sense of purpose. Without this struggle toward some degree of excellence we would lose ourselves in the monotony of mediocrity. There is more to us than what we normally accept. We frequently underestimate our capacity for godliness. We fail to stretch our humanity because our expectations are limited. We are created with a need to move onward and upward. To sense some progress on the journey is a great source of fulfillment. We have no better gauge of how we are doing than the gospel of our Lord Jesus. It tells us that nobody can be somebody and that anybody can belong to everybody in Christ Jesus. The good news is that we are "becomers," not "arrivers." The process toward achievement keep us believing there is a place for us in God's scheme of things.

Let us, therefore, never minimize the demands of Christianity. It is harder than any other lifestyle because it brings out the best within us. If we sentimentalize our faith and turn discipleship into a syrupy ceremony we miss the meaning of commitment and sacrifice. We must never try to camouflage the cross lest we lose the strength of its dying love. God gave His best to show us what is best for us. Indeed His greatest challenge to us is to be baptized with His baptism and to drink from His cup of pain. In the difficulty of our task we will find His glory.

More than Luck

There are a lot of things in life, which seem to happen with little or no explanation. We tend to call such occurrences "luck," and if they seem to defy the laws of mere chance we call them "miracles." Most of life's unexplainable events are put in one of these categories. "Luck" is often seen as the result of mere coincidence while "miracle" has providential implication. Luck can be either good or bad depending on how it affects us. The chain of events, which we call "good fortune", is seldom attributed to God. Yet, when things go bad we want to blame God or some fate that has dealt us an unkind blow.

The question is - Will we go through life trusting our luck or trusting God? If our commitment is only to luck then we have a fickle god? Luck can turn against us and wreak havoc in our lives. It is like the country song, which says, "If it were not for bad luck I'd have no luck at all." Life is full of just as many sad coincidences as happy ones. Luck-trusting people face life's unexpected surprises with little or no sense of hope or promised security.

We live on an emotional roller coaster when all we have to lean on is luck. We cannot trust life in this sinful world always to be fair. No matter how good we try to be, some folk will lie about us, turn on us and hurt us in any number of ways. Although some events can be kind to us, others can be cruel. Sooner or later luck will run out on us; and then where do we turn?

This is why we need to put our trust in something, or might we say Someone, more substantial than mere luck. It is helpful to recognize a series of events that might bring us a period of good fortune. It is tragic, however, when we lose sight of God in all our circumstances. He joins in the celebration of our successes and steadies us in the midst of our failure. He creates within us a trusting spirit so that whatever life imposes upon us of goodwill or bad we know a loving God continues to reign supreme.

minimum of frustration and a maximum of courage. He teaches us that life is more than luck. It is a commitment to all that is high and holy. It is a surrender rather than a conquest as we walk with Him each step of the way.

The Pronouncement of Work

When Adam and Eve sinned in the Garden of Eden, a part of God's response was that they and their descendants would toil and labor for their survival. There is a sense in which this pronouncement contained both judgment and grace. It had a capacity to be either a curse or a blessing. The judgment of God banished them from paradise and plunged them into a world of work. A life of ease was replaced by a life of sweat and struggle for the necessities of life. They had responsibility for their own existence with all the pains and penalties involved in being survivors.

The grace of God, however, allowed them to live and to participate in the creative process. Through the skills of their hands and the ingenuity of their minds, they could join God in productive labor. God, in His mercy, invited those created in His own image to share the dream of a better world. This dream involved a willingness to work, and it still does.

There continues to be a sense of judgment and grace about the way we earn our livelihood. The work, which we do with our hands or with our minds, has the potential to curse as well as to bless. Many of us struggle not to allow the penalties to overwhelm the rewards of our honest toil. Because "who we are" is so closely related to "what we do," frustration at work can greatly damage our egos. None of us really feel good about ourselves if our commitment and productivity are not our best.

Our work becomes a curse when we lose a sense of fulfillment in what we do. The curses of laziness, disorganization and incompetence contribute to frustration in the work place. A work ethic that demands unreasonable expectations of ourselves is equally devastating. The blessing of our labor comes from an inner awareness that in whatever honorable work we do, we are laborers together with God. We learn from Him who, after a fantastic work of creation, rested on the seventh day. Indeed, there is grace both in the way we work and in the way we relax.

Future Perspectives

Prayer of Positive Thought

Thank You, Lord for a place to begin again.
Thank You for the will to want a better way.
Thank You for the push of Your purpose
and the gift of Your grace.

You come to us with the freshness of a new day
and with the cleansing waters of a new idea.
You help us escape what time has done to us
by offering us new birth.

You teach us to look for a new heaven
and a new earth wherein dwells righteousness.
You give us courage for the living of these days
and hope for the days to come.

Thank You, Lord, that we do not stay the way we are.
We can rise above the grind of greed.
We can think Your thoughts and dream Your dreams.
We can be Your people.

Thank You, Lord that you love us
even with our feisty spirits and hateful notions.
You see beyond our pretense and our obvious sins.
Your convicting grace helps us repent.

You give us a reason to believe in ourselves
even as You condemn our fowl and faulty character.
Please accept our thanks, O Lord,
for Your redemptive interest in us.

You are the praise of our lips,
the meditation of our hearts,
and the truth that makes us free.
In You we find salvation

The Future in Perspective

Someone has said, "The future is not what it used to be." Although filled with fertile thought the author of this statement is unknown. Perhaps we could speculate as to the disposition of the person who would make such a comment.

Maybe it was a pessimist who had a dismal attitude toward the future. It may reflect someone's inability to express hope. In this person's mind the negative may dominate the positive always creating a bleak outlook. He or she may have become so disillusioned with life there is little for which to look forward. It is an unsettling way to live for those who feel the best is behind them and the future can never be what it used to be.

On the other hand, however, the comment may have come from an optimist. The statement could express great hope in the future. This person may sense that the greatest days are ahead. In this person's mind the positive always prevails over the negative creating a sense of hopeful anticipation. If the future is not what it used to be, it could be better. It is a beautiful way to live and has the backing of the scriptures which point to an end time of joy and celebration. It is a matter of faith that we trust the processes of life to lead us to God's special future.

It may be possible that the statement was made by an older person who is trying to adjust to change. The kinds of things he or she anticipated early in life are no longer a reality. The years have taken their toll and the future looks different through aging eyes. It is not a matter of the future being better or worse. It is simply different. Changing times give an older perspective a new vision. The future is not what it used to be because nothing is what it used to be.

Furthermore, the statement could have been made by a young person. It may be that young eyes do not see a future as bright as their predecessors. Youth have a way of questioning and challenging a system they feel has jeopardized their future. They also have a capacity to dream the impossible dream. They have time and health on their side. For them the future can be what they make it.

Whether optimist or pessimist, young or old, the words of a gospel song may speak best to us about the future. "Many things about tomorrow, I do not seem to understand, but I know Who holds the future and I know Who holds my hand."

About the Author

Calvin S. Metcalf (DMin), a native of Marshall, North Carolina, served faithfully as pastor and as an active participant in local and state Southern Baptist denominational missions, committees and other events. He served as pastor in churches in North Carolina, South Carolina and Tennessee and served as President of the Tennessee Baptist Convention in 1989.

He was a graduate of Mars Hill Junior College and Carson-Newman University and he held an earned doctorate degree from Southeastern Baptist Theological Seminary as well as an honorary doctorate from his alma mater, Carson-Newman University.

After retiring in 1997 from Central Baptist Church of Fountain City in Knoxville, Tennessee, Calvin received a heart transplant in January 1998. The following years were spent as supply preaching in addition to serving as interim pastor for five different churches. Before he passed away in September 2014, he was in the process of completing *Now I Read Me Down to Sleep*.

He had written and presented numerous Biblical monologs throughout his career. His other books included: *Dippers and Buckets, Jump-Starts for Thoughtful Meditation, The Greatest Gift, and Voices from the Bible*.

He and his wife, Barbara, have three children:

- Gary S. Metcalf, Corporate Director, Spiritual Care, Mountain States Health Alliance, Johnson City, TN
- Karen M. Eickhoff, Associate Pastor of Education and Families, Trinity Baptist Church, Raleigh, NC
- Tina M. Olive, Physician Recruiter, Duke Primary Care, Duke University Health System, Durham, NC

Three grandchildren: